RUSTIC ITALIAN
COOKING

RUSTIC ITALIAN
COOKING

Robert
ROSE

Rustic Italian Cooking

For complete cataloguing data, see page 6.

DESIGN AND PAGE COMPOSITION:	MATTHEWS COMMUNICATIONS DESIGN
PHOTOGRAPHY:	MARK T. SHAPIRO
ART DIRECTION/FOOD PHOTOGRAPHY:	SHARON MATTHEWS
FOOD STYLIST:	KATE BUSH
PROP STYLIST:	CHARLENE ERRICSON
MANAGING EDITOR:	PETER MATTHEWS
TEST KITCHEN:	LESLEIGH LANDRY, JAN MAIN
INDEXER:	BARBARA SCHON
COLOR SCANS & FILM:	POINTONE GRAPHICS

Cover photo: MINESTRONE TOSCANO • *TUSCAN VEGETABLE SOUP (PAGE 46)*

Distributed in the U.S. by:
Firefly Books (U.S.) Inc.
P.O. Box 1338
Ellicott Station
Buffalo, NY   14205

Distributed in Canada by:
Stoddart Publishing Co. Ltd.
34 Lesmill Road
North York, Ontario
M3B 2T6

ORDER LINES
Tel: (416) 499-8412
Fax: (416) 499-8313

ORDER LINES
Tel: (416) 213-1919
Fax: (416) 213-1917

Published by: Robert Rose Inc. • 156 Duncan Mill Road, Suite 12
Toronto, Ontario, Canada M3B 2N2   Tel: (416) 449-3535

Printed in Canada

1234567 BP 01 00 99 98

CONTENTS

Canadian Cataloguing in Publication Data

Sloan, Kathleen
    Rustic Italian cooking

Includes index.
ISBN 1-896503-98-5

1. Cookery, Italian. I. Title.

TX723.S526 1998   641.59'45   C98-931592-4

Photo Prop Credits

The author and publisher wish to express their appreciation to the following suppliers of props used in the food photography appearing in this book:

MUTI ITALIAN COUNTRY	DISHES, CUTLERY, TAPESTRIES AND ACCESSORIES
HOMEFRONT	DISHES, CUTLERY, LINENS AND ACCESSORIES
HORTICULTURAL DESIGN	PLANTS AND ACCESSORIES

Acknowledgements

Appreciative thanks to my friend Johanna Burkhard and to Bob Dees of Robert Rose who saw the special light in my eye when I spoke of Italy.

To agent extraordinaire Denise Schon for her kindness, willing ear and expertise.

A grateful thank you, to Julia Aitken for her continued friendship and support. Long may we mangia together.

To my favorite chef and good friend, Chris McDonald whose devotion to food continues to inspire me. A big thank you for introducing me to the 'Root' of Italy.

To chefs Massimo Capra and Andrew Milne Allan, two of the best, for their kind and willing help.

Grateful thanks to my friend Michael Morelli, his sister Joanne Morelli and their mother Amelia D'Agostino, whose Ristorante Paradiso in Maiorano di Monte (Caserta), Italy, defines cucina rustica.

To Kate Bush for her care, knowledge, talent and skill.

To Marian Butler for her fast and practised proofing eye and for never failing to be there when needed.

To Ben Jones, my generous and willing computer connection.

To my beautiful daughters, Alysa and Jenna King, whom I treasure more than a mountain of white truffles – for sharing my passion, and for always supporting their Mum with love.

To my widespread group of home testers and tasters, without whose help I would have finished this book at least six months late, thank you! Nora Snikvalds, Doug Boylin, Jenna King, Lori Fournier, Gail Coulthard, Jill Wilcox, Julie Cohen. Extra thanks to Mara Subotincic, Jan Main and Lesleigh Landry.

To my sweet little grandson Colsen Liam Jones, for showing such enthusiasm for his Gran's risotto, and for teaching me how to eat pasta with both hands.

To my wonderful black Lab, Casey, whose uncanny knack for knowing just when to interrupt work for the park keeps me in working order.

Lastly, and most importantly, the warmest possible gratitude to my first and finest editor, Shelley Robertson, for the first big push, for believing in me and for caring enough to show me "how to make it better."

Mille grazie.

This book is dedicated to the memory of my dear Mum,

Kathleen Hutchinson Sloan,

Who fed me first and best;

And whose culinary skills, love and reverence for good

food, simply prepared

Remain my finest inspiration

Introduction

Open my heart, and you will see

Graved inside of it, "Italy."

– Robert Browning

For me, the food of Italy is all-consuming in its appeal. It speaks directly to every one of my senses in a way no other cuisine does. Ultimately, this is food the way I think it is meant to be – natural, colorful and sensual, with layers of flavor and texture.

Splashing a little extra virgin olive oil into a warm skillet, chopping a fat, cream-colored clove of garlic, slicing through a brilliant red pepper or watching fresh chopped tomatoes turn themselves into a brilliant sauce in minutes – all these things make me feel part of the wonderful tradition of home-style Italian cooking which is such an integral part of that beautiful country.

Growing up in an Anglo-Irish household in Toronto did not precisely prepare me for writing this book. However well I was fed (and indeed I was), dishes such as roast beef, Yorkshire pudding and potato bread did not feed an appetite for rustic Italian food.

Or perhaps they did.

Whether or not she recognized it, my Mum – the most natural and instinctive of cooks – had much in common with the mothers and grandmothers of Italy and their finest cooking. As passionately and ritualistically as they produced their warming soups, slow-braised meats, handmade breads and pastas, so did she make her beef stew, shepherd's pie, blackcurrant jam and the flawless pastries for which

she was especially renowned. It matters little that she cooked with butter and not olive oil, or that she chose to make pastry and bread dough instead of pasta; her reverence for working quickly, respectfully and simply with only the very best, freshest, seasonal foods absolutely mimics *la cucina casalinga* – the home cooking of Italy I so admire.

The passion for the food itself, the inspiration to feed a family well and to never, never waste anything – "the economy of your grandmother" as Ruskin described it – such are the characteristics shared by good cooks everywhere, no matter what the ingredients with which they work.

I wrote this book because I want to contribute in some small way to reinforcing a way of cooking that I think of as simply the best. It is an opinion that, happily, is shared by the family and friends for whom I have prepared the dishes in this book.

As a food writer I have become increasingly weary of the globetrotting dinner plates too often placed before me in restaurants. When properly wrought by talented chefs who have a strong grounding in the classics, fusion cuisine is marvelous, inspiring, thrilling.

In the wrong, impatient hands, it's simply con-fusion.

Little wonder then, that I often find myself yearning for the clarity and uncontrived simplicity of the foods I so enjoyed in Italy. There, as in much of the Old World, cooking styles are not driven by trends. Not so here – perhaps because in the New World we feel the ongoing need to reinvent or reinterpret the classics.

What countries like Italy have to teach us (again and again, it would appear) is the art of culinary relaxation – how to enjoy the simplicity and clarity of rusticity, how to anticipate seasonal foods and, once they are here, respect them by allowing their "realness" to shine. This is food on a plate or in a bowl to be eaten with pleasure – no worries, no over-think.

So, this is the inspiration for RUSTIC ITALIAN COOKING, a book that features my favorite regional Italian dishes. Here you'll discover food from the haute cities of the North to the humble villages of the South and from coast to coast. This is Italian cooking at its simplest and finest: unpretentious, unchanged by time, uninfluenced by trend and, ultimately, the most satisfying – to prepare, to serve and to enjoy, again and again.

While every region in Italy has indigenous classics – each with distinct characteristics – there is an uncontrived quality that is common to food throughout the country, so preparing it successfully is a fully attainable goal. This is the sustainable cuisine that has fed Italians well for generations. It is the essence of good food – rustic, real, relevant and deeply satisfying to prepare.

I hope these recipes inspire you to cook with the same passion and excitement I feel when I cook *cucina rustica*.

Buon gusto!

Kathleen Sloan
Toronto 1998

Necessities of the Italian Pantry

To maintain the integrity of rustic Italian cooking, your pantry should be as authentic as possible. That doesn't necessarily mean a grocery shopping trip to Emilia-Romagna – however appealing the prospect! – but it does mean choosing ingredients for their quality and seasonal availability. This means cooking with ingredients like authentic Parmigiano-Reggiano, fine extra-virgin olive oil and the best dried porcini you can find. When you start with a foundation based on the best, that's generally what you end up with.

It's true that in North America we may not always as often have access to some of the mainstays taken for granted in Italy. (Although even Italian cooks are restricted by the seasonal availability of some ingredients.) The recipes contained in this book have been developed and tested on this side of the Atlantic and, with a few exceptions, are based on ingredients that are easy to find and not terribly expensive.

Here, style is all. When you are cooking with – and in – the rustic Italian style, the quality of the ingredients, the composition of the dish, the techniques used to achieve it, and the spirit with which it is presented and enjoyed all go toward making this food what it is – simply *magnifico*.

Anchovies

In Italy and other Mediterranean countries, anchovies are often salt-packed by hand in little glass jars or bottles, and are far superior to the filleted, oil-saturated canned anchovies most common in North America. They are often available in specialty food shops or in fine Italian grocers or markets. If, however, you can't find them, substitute good quality canned anchovies, rinsed of excess oil and patted dry.

Beans

Fagioli (beans) have been eaten throughout the centuries in Italy, especially in rustic country cooking. Perhaps no other culture has done as much with the humble bean as the Italians. They form the basis for soups, support main courses or meat, are tossed with pasta and, when fresh, simply eaten raw out of hand from the pod. With a few seasonal exceptions, most of the Italian varieties available in North America – like borlotti, romano, cannellini (small kidney beans) and fava (broad beans) – will have to be purchased dry, canned or frozen; using any of these will yield good results with all of the dishes in this book that call for beans. If I can't have fresh, my preference is for dry beans that are soaked overnight and cooked. An alternative to the overnight soaking method is the quick-soak-and-boil method which is explained on packages of dry beans. If you choose canned beans, rinse them well before using.

Butter

Although not generally associated with Italian cooking, butter is a staple of the Northern Italian larder and shows up in a number of recipes from that part of the country. Risotto recipes, for instance, call for a combination of a little (unsalted) butter and olive oil. If you use salted butter, use less salt in the recipe. Often a small knob of butter is added at the last moment to enrich sauces that are teamed with pasta.

Cheese

Life is too short to cook with inferior cheese. And Italy's world famous cheeses lend so much authenticity, quality and taste to the dishes in which they are featured that it is worth the little extra cost they may demand. Even so, a little goes a long way. And it's better to use 1 to 2 oz (25 to 50 g) of authentic Parmigiano-Reggiano than an entire canister of that strange ready-grated cheese that dares to call itself "Parmesan." Whenever possible, buy imported Italian cheese in pieces from a good cheesemonger (the nice bonus here is that you can also sample before you buy!) or a better-quality supermarket.

There are many wonderful cheeses from Italy (I mention but a few here), and these are generally classified as either hard, semi-hard or soft.

Authentic **Parmigiano-Reggiano** (which can only be produced in the Emilia Romagna region) is, I think, the world's greatest cheese. And not just for grating. Try it at room temperature, cut into rough chunks or shaved thin, drizzled with extra virgin olive oil, then scattered with cracked black pepper, along with a glass of strong red wine. Or try it at the end of a meal with a fresh, ripe pear – nirvana, Italian-style! Yes, it costs a little more but yes, there is a difference.

Also look for **Grana Padano**, another hard Italian cheese that is also made from cow's milk and, like Parmigiano-Reggiano, is suitable for grating. In some cases, you can also use it as a less expensive substitute for Parmigiano Reggiano.

Pecorino Romano is another hard cheese, but made from sheep's milk. It is used grated or shaved when it reaches tangy maturity and is the cheese of choice in Southern Italy where the largest numbers of sheep graze. **Mozzarella** needs no introduction to North Americans, although I urge you to taste the difference between supermarket-wrapped mozzarella and the real thing.

Mascarpone is a soft cream cheese made to be consumed soon after purchasing; it is used usually, but not exclusively, in sweets and desserts.

Ricotta is another soft cheese whose name translates as "cooked twice." There are a number of versions in Italy that range from quite soft to a hard salted variety known as *ricotta salata* which is used grated. **Fontina** is the queen of Piedmont's Aosta Valley, a full-fat semi-soft cheese with a pungent, nutty flavor and the ability to melt to a lustrous smoothness – quite wonderful.

Gorgonzola is Italy's tribute to blue cheese, a cow's milk cheese beautifully suited to many applications or simply enjoyed with fresh fruit.

Garlic

Look for small heads of ultra-fresh garlic with tight heads, firm cloves, no soft spots and definitely no green shoots. The oversized elephant garlic doesn't have the depth of flavor required for classic Italian cooking – and it doesn't seem to fill the kitchen with that wonderful aroma that declares great food is in the works! As for ready-chopped garlic packed in oil – well, the less said about it the better.

Herbs

While I know many home cooks who use dried herbs with success, I recommend using fresh herbs whenever possible. To me, there is simply no comparison. Considering the difference between fresh and dry herbs is a little like comparing grapes with raisins or fresh tomatoes with sun-dried – entirely different creatures. Basil, rosemary, marjoram, oregano, thyme, sage and flat-leaf parsley are ubiquitous throughout recipes in this book, and their flavors do make such a difference. Still, if you must use dried herbs, be sure to reduce the amount. (Generally the rule is 1 tsp [5 mL] of dry to 1 tbsp [15 mL] of fresh.) Rub the dried herbs between your fingers before adding to the recipe.

Mushrooms

In Italy, mushrooms and *porcini* seem to be more-or-less synonymous. But in North America the closest we can usually come to porcini is the dried variety. Far from being a poor substitute, however, fine-quality dried porcini are a valuable, prized ingredient. A few ounces can go a long way towards positively influencing a larger quantity (say, 8 oz [250 g]) of domestic mushrooms. Also good is a combination of fresh "wild" mushrooms (such as chanterelles, oyster mushrooms, horn-of-plenty or morels) or the little brown cremini mushrooms, combined with rehydrated porcini.

Nuts

Unless you have a good source for shelled nuts (organic stores and bulk shops often sell good quality, fresh shelled nuts), buy nuts in the shell for these recipes. It doesn't take long to shell them and the difference in taste can be dramatic. I like to purchase pine nuts loose rather than in those expensive little bottles; this way, I can taste one for freshness and I can buy just what I need. When toasting nuts (in an oven or a skillet) make sure to be attentive; they can burn quickly, making them unusable.

Olive oil

The lifeblood that flows through Italy's food, olive oil is to the Italian kitchen what butter is to the French kitchen – an important distinction being that olive oil is reputed to be a beneficial fat. There is much that has been written about this ancient oil, but here is all you need to know: Keep at least two types in your pantry. The more expensive cold-pressed extra virgin olive oil is top-quality oil from the olive's first pressing. Because of its cost – and low smoking point – it is less appropriate for cooking than dressing vegetables, salads, as a partner to good bread or as a final touch drizzled over some soups. Good quality virgin olive oil is from the second and third pressing (sometimes graded "fine" or "medium fine") and is still of above-average quality; use it for sauces and other cooking. Depending on the brand, olive oil labeled "pure olive oil" or sometimes simply "olive oil" is good for shallow and deep-frying. Many Italian food stores and other fine food shops offer a variety of olive oil tastings from time to time. This is a great way to experience the difference in extra virgin olive oils, whether fruity, peppery, mellow, "green" or robust. I am not a fan of store-bought flavored olive oils.

Pancetta

Pancetta is unsmoked Italian bacon; it is widely available, sold rolled and pre-sliced in many supermarkets or at the deli counter. It is bacon cured from pork belly and, because it is unsmoked, it does not intrude with unwanted extra flavor. "Green" (or unsmoked) conventional bacon can be used as a substitute in the recipes presented here.

Pasta

With a couple of exceptions, the pasta recipes in this book were tested with store-bought dried pasta. My own brand preference is for Rustichella d'Abruzzo, which is made from stoneground durum wheat and imported from Italy. (I also like De Cecco and Barilla.) But as long as you don't overcook it (this is so critical), any brand will do. There are a couple of cardinal rules that apply to cooking dried pasta: Add it to a large amount of boiling water, then add the salt; give it one good stir and allow to cook until firm but tender – *al dente*. Remember it will continue to cook slightly after removing it from the water. Drain quickly – never rinse – and allow a little of the cooking water to cling to the pasta. This is very important as it allows the pasta to be coated evenly with the sauce; if you dry out the cooked pasta over heat the sauce will slide off. Whenever possible, add the cooked pasta to the sauce in the skillet. This is the Italian way, which ensures the pasta is coated with the sauce and everything arrives at the table hot.

Pepper

Freshly ground pepper is imperative. So if you don't have one already, invest in a pepper mill. I use a combination of black and white peppercorns in mine.

Polenta

Coarsley ground yellow cornmeal or polenta single-handedly defines rustic Italian cooking for me. As simple as this staple is, it can be transformed with little effort into something really great. In short, you can dress it up and take it anywhere.

There are a number of categories of polenta or cornmeal – regular or coarse grained, stoneground coarse, pre-made polenta (which I wouldn't recommend) and instant polenta (which I would). Die-hard polenta aficionados maintain that if it doesn't require a labor-intensive 20 minutes or so to make, it ain't real polenta. But I often enjoy the smoothness and overall quality of the imported instant polenta (I especially like Beretta Express, which, happily, has a slightly coarser grain than many other instant varieties) not to mention the fact that it is ready in 5 to 6 minutes. Even those who say they are not fond of polenta will go for it when it is made from fine-grained cornmeal. The preference is personal but generally speaking, use a finer ground cornmeal when planning to make creamy polenta and a coarser one when you want to make a set polenta suitable for grilling or pan-frying. The coarser polenta will always require a little longer cooking time.

Prosciutto

Parma's gift to the world's table, original Italian prosciutto has not always been as widely available in North America as it is now. Cured only with salt and the special breezes unique to this area's mountain region, prosciutto has been made in Italy for more than 2,000 years. Italian prosciutto is cured for more than one year at controlled temperatures, using carefully regulated procedures. If you are committed to using the best Italian-made prosciutto, look for the stamp of approval issued by the inspectors of the Agency for Parma Quality Certification. This stamp – a five-pointed ducal crown – ensures authentic original prosciutto. When cooking with prosciutto, be careful not to overcook or it will toughen, making it much less appealing.

Rice

Short-grained Arborio, grown exclusively in Italy's northern regions, is the rice of choice for risotto and even some desserts in Italy. There are four different varieties: *ordinario*, the shortest grain; *semifino*; *fino*, a medium-length grain; and finally, *superfino*, the finest and largest of them all. Plump-grained and snowy white, Arborio rice is revered for its special properties; because of its high starch content, it is the only short-grain rice recommended for risotto, the classic dish of the northern Italian kitchen. Its size enables it to absorb lots of cooking liquid while developing an ultra-creamy quality, yet it always retains its true, firm heart – what the Italians call *all'onda* or waviness. The late food writer Bert Greene described it thusly: "each kernel manages to stay afloat and firm in a virtual sea of flavor." That, in essence, is risotto, which you simply cannot make with any other rice.

Salt

Sea salt, both coarse and finely ground is the preferred variety. Iodized salt leaves an unpleasant flavor.

Tomatoes

Let me make one thing perfectly clear about tomatoes – in cooking it is better to use good quality canned tomatoes (preferably San Marzano plum tomatoes, imported from Italy) than 1 lb (500 g) of fresh tomatoes of inferior quality. If fresh, ripe plum tomatoes (also called Italian plum tomatoes) are available, by all means use them. If they are not, or if you are not in the mood to prepare them for cooking, feel free to use canned, peeled plum tomatoes. For many of the recipes in this book I have mentioned *passata*, which is a simple preparation of puréed tomatoes that have been cooked briefly and finely strained. You may find authentic imported Italian *passata* in tall glass bottles in Italian groceries and in some supermarkets. There are also good North American supermarket versions available now. However, canned (or fresh) plum tomatoes chopped and sautéed until thickened (in olive oil with a little garlic, salt and freshly ground black pepper) is a perfect substitute. This simple sauce forms the backbone for so many Italian dishes. I provide alternatives within the recipes but by all means experiment and use what works for you.

Domestic tomato sauces packed in jars – notwithstanding their Italianate names and images of happy peasants at work in the fields – are poor substitutes, too often sugared or over-salted, with the addition of nasty dry herbs and grated cheese. For goodness sake, pass these by. They have no place in authentic Italian cooking.

Canned tomato products you may want to experiment with include simple canned plum tomatoes in their juice, canned plum tomatoes chunked in tomato sauce, tomato purée, ground or crushed tomatoes, as well as tomatoes in tomato paste. Occasionally I use tomato paste (buy the best you can afford) for thickening. But I rarely use it along with any of the above tomato preparations. On one of my trips to Italy, I brought back a jar of *estratto di pomodoro*, which is a wonderfully dark paste with a spreadable consistency, made from sun-dried tomatoes; however, I have yet to find it in North America.

Finally, there are sun-dried tomatoes, the valuable little item that has suffered the same North American overkill that afflicted New Zealand kiwi fruit in the 1980's. However, used within the context of authentic Italian cooking, they shine. If you buy sun-dried tomatoes that are not packed in olive oil, enliven them by covering them with extra virgin olive oil and allow to rehydrate for a day.

Vinegar

Aceto Balsamico Tradizionale di Modena is true balsamic vinegar – a dark, dense elixir with a hypnotically aromatic flavor that owes its superiority and high price to the fact that it is made entirely from white Trebbiano grapes and aged for years in a series of different wood casks. Its rich, deeply intense flavor is prized as highly as good wine for imparting depth and character to sauces, grilled vegetables and meats, for deglazing pans or even to splash over ripe strawberries or melon. Once again, buy the highest quality you can afford. At the very least, look for imported-from-Italy balsamic vinegar that has been aged for a minimum of six years. In Modena, you will find kegs of balsamic vinegar that are almost 100 years old. Expensive? Absolutely. So when someone says they have fallen in love with you and they want to buy you something to commemorate their love, tell them you want the best *aceto balsamico* they can find. Accept no substitute.

Mangia poco, bene, e spesso

*E*at little, well and often…these words are the inspiration for this book and, I believe, for the traditional style in which Italians eat. I have organized the chapters to follow the traditional order of the Italian meal. If you choose to adhere to this dictum, you can enjoy a varied assortment of foods, with smaller portions of each course – and without fear of overindulging.

ANTIPASTI

Olivada • *Black Olive Pâté* 21

Focaccia alla Salvia • *Sage Bread* 22

Caponata • *Sicilian Eggplant Relish* 24

Fett'unta al Pomodoro • *Tuscan Garlic Tomato Bread* 26

Peperonata • *Sautéed Peppers, Tomato and Onion* 27

Crostini di Fegato di Pollo • *Chicken Liver Crostini* 28

Fagioli Bianchi alla Menta • *White Bean with Mint* 29

Peperoni Arrostiti con Parmigiano-Reggiano • *Roasted Red Pepper with Parmigiano-Reggiano* 29

Frittata di Menta • *Open-Faced Omelette with Fresh Mint* 30

Cipolline in Agrodolce • *Sweet-and-Sour Onions* 31

Zucca in Agrodolce • *Squash Marinated in Red Wine Vinegar* 32

Salvia Fritta • *Deep-Fried Fresh Sage* 33

Fonduta • *Melted Fontina Cheese* 34

Torta di Spinaci • *Spinach Pie* 35

Rustici • *Stuffed Puff Pastries* 36

In Italian, *pasto* means "meal" – hence *antipasto* means "before the meal." For me, the essence of antipasto is in simple savory dishes, creatively conceived. Here the emphasis is on rustic breads like focaccia, as well as vegetable preparations based on vibrantly colored peppers, eggplant and tomato. Other small delights include new onions in balsamic vinegar or fresh beans with shrimp and mint, a splendid Italian gratin of potatoes, tomatoes and cheese, or a herb-flecked frittata. These are all antipasto.

The beauty of these classic dishes is magnified by their versatility; they are small meals and, as such, are perfect for lunches, light dinners or as part of an impressive Italian buffet. Many of them – especially the vegetable dishes – are best enjoyed at room temperature, making them even more user-friendly.

My first taste of black olive "pâté" was not in Italy but at Trattoria Giancarlo, a Toronto restaurant. I marvelled then, as I do now, at how something can be so astoundingly simple and so astoundingly good.

This versatile mixture is wonderful tossed with fresh, hot pasta. You can also try it as a topping for grilled fish or chicken, or as an omelette filling.

Don't choose kalamata olives for this preparation, as they are just a little too bitter.

Allow the pâté to come to room temperature before serving as a spread.

You can vary the recipe by adding a few sun-dried tomatoes, roasted red peppers, grilled eggplant or 1 or 2 dried chilies.

A jar of this makes a wonderful gift for olive lovers.

Olivada

Black Olive Pâté

1 cup	pitted black olives, preferably oil-cured	250 mL
4	sprigs flat-leaf parsley	4
2 tbsp	fresh bread crumbs	25 mL
1 tbsp	butter	15 mL
1 1/2 tsp	grated lemon zest	7 mL
2 tbsp	lemon juice	25 mL
2 tbsp	extra virgin olive oil	25 mL
	Salt and freshly ground black pepper	
6	slices rustic country-style bread	6
	Olive oil	

1. In a food processor, combine olives, parsley, bread crumbs, butter, lemon zest, lemon juice and olive oil; blend until a smooth paste forms. (Alternatively, with a sharp chef's knife, finely chop olives, parsley, bread crumbs and lemon zest; transfer to a bowl and blend in butter, lemon juice and olive oil.) Season to taste with salt and pepper.

2. Brush bread slices with a little olive oil. Grill or toast until golden. Spread each slice with about 2 tbsp (25 mL) of the *olivada*. Serve immediately.

I have experimented with a number of recipes for focaccia, the definitive rustic-style, leavened bread with seemingly endless variations. Many call for a yeast and flour sponge or starter dough (called a biga) to be made ahead of time and used as a central ingredient blended with more yeast and flour. This is a good idea in Italy and Europe (where the flour is weaker than in North America), since it strengthens the basic flour mixture. While this simplified version omits the biga, it provides wonderfully traditional results.

Be sure to use fresh sage for this recipe; dried sage tends to discolor the dough.

You can enrich the interior of the bread – or just the surface – with fresh herbs and cheeses. But the combinations of toppings and fillings for focacce are endless. Black olives, garlic, onion, red peppers, anchovies and tomatoes can all be used with or without freshly grated cheese. I've even enjoyed a sweet breakfast focaccia studded with fat raisins and dusted with sugar.

Focaccia alla Salvia

Sage Bread

15- BY 10-INCH (40 BY 25 CM) RIMMED BAKING SHEET, LIGHTLY OILED AND DUSTED WITH FLOUR

3 tbsp	extra virgin olive oil	45 mL
1	large onion, finely chopped	1
3	cloves garlic, minced	3
1/2 cup	chopped fresh sage	125 mL
	Salt and freshly ground black pepper	
Pinch	granulated sugar	Pinch
1	pkg active dry yeast (or 2 1/2 tsp [12 mL])	1
2 tsp	salt	10 mL
2 tsp	granulated sugar	10 mL
1 cup	lukewarm milk	250 mL
6 to 7 cups	all-purpose flour	1.5 to 1.75 L
	Extra virgin olive oil for brushing	
	Coarse salt for sprinkling	
1/2 cup	whole fresh sage leaves	125 mL

1. In a skillet heat olive oil over medium heat. Add onion and garlic; cook for 5 minutes or until softened. Do not let garlic brown. Stir in chopped sage; cook 1 minute longer. Season to taste with salt and pepper. Cool.

2. Warm a small bowl with hot tap water; drain. In warmed bowl, dissolve pinch of sugar in 1/2 cup (125 mL) lukewarm water. Sprinkle in yeast; let stand 10 minutes or until frothy.

3. In a large bowl, combine onion mixture, yeast mixture, salt, sugar, lukewarm milk and 1 cup (250 mL) lukewarm water. Stir in flour, 1 cup (250 mL) at a time, until soft dough forms. On a lightly floured surface, knead dough for 5 minutes or until smooth and elastic, adding enough of remaining flour to keep dough from sticking.

4. Transfer dough to a large, oiled bowl. Turn dough to coat with oil. Cover with plastic wrap, then a clean tea towel. Let rise in a warm place for 2 hours or until doubled in size and indentations remain when dough is poked with two fingers. Punch dough down, cover and let rise for 1 hour.

5. Transfer dough to lightly floured work surface and divide into 2 pieces. Pulling and stretching, begin to work the dough into the shape of a rectangle. Place on prepared baking sheet and continue to pull and stretch the dough to a size of about 10 by 4 inches (25 by 10 cm). Repeat procedure with second piece of dough. Leave pan in a warm place for about 45 minutes to allow dough to rise.

6. Preheat oven to 450° F (230° C). When dough has risen, make fairly deep indentations across the surface with your fingers. Brush generously with olive oil, sprinkle coarse salt over the surface and place in middle of preheated oven for about 30 minutes or until crisp and deep golden brown. Remove from oven; cool on a rack. Scatter fresh sage leaves over surface of each, cut into squares and serve.

Caponata

Sicilian Eggplant Relish

SERVES 6 TO 8

A tradition in Sicily where eggplant is ubiquitous, caponata is an incredibly versatile vegetable dish and perhaps the finest example of Italian antipasti. There are endless contemporary variations of this dish, but in Sicily two ingredients remain constant – eggplant and celery. Serve at room temperature with good bread and cheese or alongside grilled sausages, fish or chicken or even tossed with pasta.

Here I have chosen to toss the eggplant chunks with a little olive oil and oven-roast them instead of frying. This method is more convenient and more in keeping with contemporary tastes, since the eggplant absorbs less oil. In fact, you can roast all of the fresh vegetables to create a thoroughly contemporary caponata.

If you choose to sauté the eggplant, make sure your olive oil is hot enough to sear it – otherwise it will absorb too much oil.

I have had success with this recipe using all three varieties of eggplant – conventional, globe, as well as the slender purple Asian type.

Toast the pine nuts in a pan on top of the stove or in a preheated oven, but keep your eye on them, as they will brown very quickly.

LARGE BAKING SHEET

3 lbs	eggplant, trimmed and cut into 1-inch (2.5 cm) cubes	1.5 kg
2 tbsp	salt	25 mL
1/3 cup	olive oil	75 mL
4	stalks celery, trimmed, cut diagonally into 1/2-inch (1 cm) pieces, blanched	4
4	cloves garlic, minced	4
2	medium onions, thinly sliced	2
2 cups	*passata* (puréed, sieved tomatoes) *or* canned Italian plum tomatoes, drained and chopped	500 mL
1/2 cup	large green olives, pitted and roughly chopped	125 mL
1/2 cup	black olives, pitted and roughly chopped	125 mL
3 tbsp	capers (preferably salt-packed, rinsed)	45 mL
2 tbsp	pine nuts, lightly toasted	25 mL
2 tbsp	currants, soaked in hot water for 15 minutes, drained and patted dry	25 mL
2 tbsp	granulated sugar	25 mL
1/4 cup	balsamic vinegar	50 mL
	Salt and freshly ground black pepper	
1/2 cup	roughly chopped mint	125 mL
1/2 cup	roughly chopped basil	125 mL

1. Put cubed eggplant in a colander set in the sink. Toss with the salt. Set a plate on top of eggplant and add a weight. Let stand 1 hour. Preheat oven to 400° F (200° C). Rinse eggplant under cold running water; drain and pat dry with paper towel. Toss eggplant with 3 tbsp (45 mL) of the olive oil; spread onto baking sheet and bake for 20 minutes, stirring occasionally, or until softened and starting to brown. Set aside.

2. In a large skillet, heat remaining olive oil over medium heat. Add celery, garlic and onions; cook for 6 minutes or until onions are softened. Do not let garlic brown. Sir in *passata*, green and black olives, capers, pine nuts, currants, sugar and vinegar. Season to taste with salt and pepper. Reduce heat to medium-low and cook for 15 minutes or until vegetables are tender.

3. Stir in mint; cook 5 minutes longer. Transfer to large serving dish. Let stand at room temperature 2 hours to develop flavors. Serve at room temperature, sprinkled with chopped basil.

Fett'unta and bruschetta are much the same, each based on good country-style bread, sliced and grilled or toasted. Here we find the essence of rustic Italian eating – something that could only have been conceived in a country with such an abiding love for olive oil and tomatoes.

If you can toast the bread over a wood-burning fire, so much the better. And don't even think of making this Tuscan specialty with anything other than the ripest, heftiest plum tomatoes. Try to use an olive oil with a green, peppery quality. This recipe is easily doubled or tripled.

Fett'unta al Pomodoro

Tuscan Garlic Tomato Bread

3	large ripe plum tomatoes	3
6	thick slices of rustic country-style bread	6
3	large cloves garlic, peeled and cut in half	3
1/4 cup	extra virgin olive oil	50 mL
	Salt and freshly ground black pepper to taste	

1. Cut the tomatoes in half and squeeze to remove seeds and juice.

2. Toast or grill the bread until lightly browned. Rub one side of each bread slice with a half clove of garlic. Then roughly rub a deseeded tomato half over the same side of the bread until the bread begins to take on the color and the essence of the tomato. Repeat procedure with remaining bread, garlic and tomato.

3. Place bread on a serving platter. Drizzle with the olive oil and season each slice with salt and pepper.

Peperonata

Sautéed Peppers, Tomato and Onion

SERVES 4 TO 6

Slow-cooked peppers, tomatoes and onions result in peperonata, *a classic Italian preparation that captures the vibrant flavors of summer-ripe vegetables. In Tuscany, they enjoy this dish with the addition of potatoes; in Sicily, they add huge green olives. But here, in this simple recipe, I've chosen to "do as the Romans do."*

Serve with roast pork, veal or grilled sausages, with pasta, in sandwiches, as part of an antipasti table, as a crostini topping or with egg dishes.

1/4 cup	olive oil	50 mL
3	cloves garlic, chopped	3
2	large red onions, sliced	2
2	large red bell peppers, cut into strips	2
1	large green pepper, cut into strips	1
1	large yellow or orange bell pepper, cut into strips	1
2	large ripe plum tomatoes, peeled, seeded and roughly chopped	2
1/4 cup	chopped flat-leaf parsley	50 mL
2 tbsp	balsamic or red wine vinegar	25 mL
	Salt and freshly ground black pepper	

1. In a large, heavy-bottomed skillet, warm the olive oil over medium heat. Add garlic and onions; cook, stirring occasionally, for 10 minutes or until softened.

2. Add sliced peppers; stir to coat with oil, adding a little more olive oil if necessary. Cook, stirring occasionally, for 20 minutes or until vegetables are tender and beginning to brown.

3. Stir in tomatoes, parsley, vinegar and salt and pepper to taste. Cook 10 minutes longer, stirring occasionally. Serve at room temperature.

SERVES 6 TO 8

Crostini are, strictly speaking, thin slices of bread that have been brushed with olive oil and grilled or toasted. However, this name also applies to the inventive little appetizers – not unlike canapés – you get when these little toasts are treated to a variety of toppings. In fact, the definition of crostini can be expected to include grilled polenta squares, ciabatta, focaccia and mini pancakes based on chickpea flour or potatoes – all serving as platforms for a myriad of toppings. At Mistura in Toronto, Chef Massimo Capra offers a wonderful assortment of crostini on his decidedly authentic Italian menu. Grilled radicchio, mushrooms, artichoke, olivada, strips of authentic Italian prosciutto and, of course, fresh tomato all make typically good crostini. Here are three favorite toppings.

Crostini di Fegato di Pollo

Chicken Liver Crostini

2 tbsp	olive oil	25 mL
1 tbsp	butter	15 mL
1	small onion, finely chopped	1
2	cloves garlic, minced	2
1 tbsp	chopped flat-leaf parsley	15 mL
1 tbsp	chopped fresh sage	15 mL
1 tbsp	capers	15 mL
	Salt and freshly ground black pepper to taste	
12 oz	chicken livers, trimmed and quartered	375 g
1/4 cup	Marsala or Vin Santo *or* white wine	50 mL
	Softened butter as needed	

1. In a skillet, heat olive oil and butter over medium heat. Add onion and garlic; cook for 5 minutes or until softened. Stir in parsley, sage, capers and salt and pepper to taste; cook for 3 minutes.

2. Stir in chicken livers and wine; cook for 10 minutes or until cooked through, stirring occasionally and adding a little water if necessary to keep livers from drying out.

3. Transfer mixture to food processor or blender; process until smooth, adding enough softened butter to achieve spreading consistency. Adjust seasoning to taste. Use to top crostini.

Blanch mint and parsley leaves in boiling water for 10 seconds; remove immediately and drain.

Fagioli Bianchi alla Menta

White Bean with Mint

1 cup	whole mint leaves, blanched and drained	250 mL
1 cup	whole flat-leaf parsley leaves, blanched and drained	250 mL
4	cloves garlic, peeled	4
1 1/2 cups	cooked *cannellini* beans (white kidney beans)	375 mL
2 tbsp	extra virgin olive oil	25 mL
	Salt and freshly ground black pepper	

1. In a food processor, combine mint and parsley with garlic; process until finely chopped. Add beans; process for 1 minute or until well-combined, scraping down sides of bowl at halfway point. Add oil; process until smooth.

2. Season to taste with salt and pepper. Use to top crostini.

Peperoni Arrostiti con Parmigiano-Reggiano

Roasted Red Pepper with Parmigiano-Reggiano

2	red bell peppers, roasted, seeded and peeled	2
2 tbsp	extra virgin olive oil	25 mL
6 oz	Parmigiano-Reggiano, shaved	175 g

1. In a food processor, purée the roasted peppers until smooth, adding the olive oil in a thin stream as they are being processed.

2. Use to top crostini, then add a curl or two of shaved Parmigiano-Reggiano.

The Italians use fresh mint in so many imaginative ways, and with so many different types of food: onions, eggplant, tomatoes, in sauces – even with eggs, as in this delightful frittata. Serve this drizzled with a bit of extra virgin olive oil and fresh tomatoes that have been chopped and tossed with more mint, a little sugar and balsamic vinegar.

Swiss chard or peppery greens like rapini are often used as frittata fillings, as are thin asparagus, artichoke hearts and zucchini flowers.

A thinner version of frittata, called frittatine, is almost crêpe-like in its consistency. It is filled with a variety of fresh herbs – oregano, basil, mint, sage, parsley – and, after cooking, is cut into thin strips, tossed in a delicate vinaigrette and added to salad greens with tomatoes to make a beautiful summer lunch.

Frittata di Menta

Open-Faced Omelette with Fresh Mint

3 tbsp	olive oil	45 mL
1	onion, finely chopped	1
1 cup	whole fresh mint leaves, washed and dried thoroughly	250 mL
1/4 cup	chopped flat-leaf parsley	50 mL
8	eggs	8
3 tbsp	fresh bread crumbs	45 mL
3 tbsp	grated Pecorino Romano	45 mL
2 tsp	light (10%) cream	10 mL
2 tsp	all-purpose flour	10 mL
1/2 tsp	salt	2 mL
1/4 tsp	freshly ground black pepper	1 mL

1. In a large ovenproof skillet, heat 4 tsp (20 mL) of the olive oil over medium heat. Add onion and cook for 6 minutes or until softened. Remove from heat. Stir in mint and parsley. Transfer to a bowl. Wipe skillet clean with paper towel.

2. In another bowl, whisk together eggs, bread crumbs, Pecorino Romano, cream, flour, salt and pepper. Stir in cooled onion-herb mixture.

3. Preheat broiler. Return skillet to medium heat. Add remaining olive oil, swirling to coat surface of skillet. Pour egg mixture into skillet; cook, gently running a narrow metal spatula around the edges to lift cooked egg up and allow uncooked egg to run beneath for 5 minutes or until frittata is set and cooked on the bottom.

4. Place skillet 6 inches (15 cm) beneath broiler. Cook 2 minutes or until top is set and golden brown. Serve immediately or cooled to room temperature, cut into squares or strips.

SERVES 8 TO 10

Agrodolce *translates as "sweet and sour," a cooking style the Italians especially like to apply to* cipolline *– small, flat, dense and exceedingly sweet little onions. While you can make this recipe successfully with small new cooking onions or pearl onions, make an effort to look for* cipolline; *they're usually sold in net bags at specialty produce markets and some supermarkets. They cost a little more – but the taste is worth it.*

The addition of fresh mint is not traditional but it works wonderfully well with the influence of the balsamic vinegar. Add the red wine if the balsamic vinegar is of average quality. If, however, you have invested in a good quality aceto balsamico, *aged 8 years or more, omit the wine.*

While blanching onions, be sure not to leave them in the boiling water longer than the allotted time or they will become too soft. They should be only slightly cooked since they will cook further with the remaining ingredients.

Cipolline in Agrodolce

Sweet-and-Sour Onions

2 lbs	*cipolline* (small new onions) or pearl onions	1 kg
2 tbsp	butter	25 mL
2 tbsp	olive oil	25 mL
1/4 cup	balsamic vinegar	50 mL
1 tbsp	granulated sugar	15 mL
3 tbsp	robust red wine (optional)	45 mL
1/4 cup	chopped fresh mint	50 mL
	Salt and freshly ground black pepper to taste	

1. Blanch onions, skins on, in boiling water for exactly 3 minutes. Remove immediately and place in cold water; remove skins.

2. In a large skillet, heat butter and olive oil over medium heat. Add onions and cook, stirring occasionally, for 5 minutes or until they start to brown.

3. Stir in vinegar, sugar and, if using, red wine. Increase heat to high and cook, stirring, for 3 minutes or until thick and syrupy. Stir in mint. Season to taste with salt and pepper. Transfer to serving dish. Serve at room temperature.

SERVES 4 TO 6

Andrew Milne Allan, chef of Toronto's Zucca Trattoria, provided this recipe for an article I wrote devoted to pumpkins. The chef's words describe it best: "This is a simple preparation on its own or as part of a mixed vegetable antipasto for one of those last fall barbecues."

Zucca is Italian for squash or pumpkin. And for sheer culinary inventiveness with this vegetable, the Italians lead the way. The inhabitants of Ferrara have been nicknamed magnazoca, or "pumpkin eaters," because of the pumpkin-stuffed pasta pillows – cappellacci – they enjoy as the first course of their traditional Christmas Eve dinner. The Mantuan town of Villastrada throws an annual pumpkin festival where the specialty is a creamy pumpkin-flavored rice dish, riso e zucca, topped with slices of fried pumpkin.

Zucca in Agrodolce

Squash Marinated in Red Wine Vinegar

1	small pumpkin, butternut or buttercup squash (about 2 1/2 lbs [1.25 kg])	1
2 tbsp	olive oil	25 mL
1/4 cup	loosely packed mint leaves	50 mL
3 tbsp	red wine vinegar	45 mL
1	clove garlic, minced	1
	Salt	

1. Cut pumpkin in half and remove peel and seeds. Cut flesh into 1/2-inch (1 cm) slices or strips. In a large saucepan of boiling salted water, cook pumpkin for 1 minute. Drain well and pat dry. Arrange pumpkin on a large platter and brush lightly with 1 tsp (5 mL) of the olive oil.

2. Preheat barbecue to medium. Cook pumpkin on greased grill for 5 minutes on each side until tender and starting to char. Return pumpkin to platter. Sprinkle with remaining oil, mint leaves, vinegar, garlic and salt to taste.

3. Let pumpkin cool in this marinade, turning slices gently once or twice before serving. Serve at room temperature.

LEFT: CAPONATA • *SICILIAN EGGPLANT RELISH* (PAGE 24) ➤
UPPER RIGHT: FETT'UNTA AL POMODORO • *TUSCAN GARLIC TOMATO BREAD* (PAGE 26)

Although these crispy little savories are often enjoyed in Italy as a digestif at the end of a meal, I think of them as a wonderful appetizer.

The etymology of salvia (sage) is "sacred herb." Tuscans adore fresh sage (as do all Italians), using it in antipasto dishes like this one, with baked polenta, in beans or with veal – even in a little-known baked custard dessert called salviata. Look for ultra-fresh sage with broad silvery green leaves, preferably from an organic herb grower.

You can vary this centuries-old recipe somewhat by adding a filling; just sandwich pairs of sage leaves with either a small bit of mozzarella or a smear of anchovy paste, then batter and fry them. Use vegetable oil or olive oil for frying.

Salvia Fritta

Deep-Fried Fresh Sage

1/2 cup	all-purpose flour	125 mL
1/2 tsp	salt	2 mL
1 tbsp	extra virgin olive oil	15 mL
2	egg whites, beaten until stiff	2
	Vegetable oil *or* olive oil for frying	
36	fresh sage leaves, washed and dried	36

1. In a small bowl, whisk together flour, salt, olive oil and 1/4 cup (50 mL) cold water until smooth. Whisk in one-third of the egg whites; fold in remaining egg whites.

2. In a large skillet, heat 1 inch (2.5 cm) of oil over medium-high heat to 350° F (180° C). In 3 batches, dip sage leaves into the batter; transfer to skillet and fry 2 minutes, turning once. When golden and crisp, remove from oil and drain on paper towel. Serve immediately.

Fonduta

Melted Fontina Cheese

SERVES 4

Melted cheese with toasted bread might sound a somewhat pedestrian affair – that is, until you realize the cheese in question is Italy's renowned fontina, whose sweet, nutty taste and pungent aroma is often described as reminiscent of tri-fola d'Alba, Piedmont's renowned white truffles. As the name suggests, fonduta is Italy's version of Alpine fondue, but with the distinctive addition of butter, milk and egg yolks.

If you don't have a double boiler, improvise one with a small saucepan placed inside a larger one filled with water. Allow at least 8 hours for the cheese to steep and soften in the milk.

Other countries produce respectable fontina – including Switzerland, Denmark, France and Canada – but for this particular dish, nothing but the Italian variety will really do.

Italian fontina is produced exclusively in the Piedmont province of Valle d'Aosta which, by happy coincidence, is also polenta and white truffle country. There, authentic fonduta is served in individual soup plates, sometimes over baked polenta slices and adorned with paper-thin shavings of those famous white truffles.

1 lb	Italian fontina, diced	500 g
1 cup	milk	250 mL
1/4 cup	butter	50 mL
4	egg yolks	4
	Grilled or toasted rustic country-style bread *or* baked slices of polenta	
	White pepper	
	Shavings of white truffle (optional)	

1. In a bowl combine diced fontina and milk. Cover and refrigerate for 8 hours or overnight.

2. In the top of a double boiler placed over hot (but not boiling) water, melt the butter. Take the bowl of milk and fontina and pour half of the milk into a smaller bowl; set aside. Add remaining milk and cheese to the melted butter. Cook, stirring with a wooden spoon, for 10 minutes or until the cheese is smooth and completely melted.

3. Beat reserved milk into egg yolks. Stir into melted cheese; cook, stirring, for 5 minutes or until thickened, smooth and creamy.

4. Place the toasted bread or thick slices of polenta in shallow soup plates. Pour the *fonduta* over bread, sprinkle with white pepper to taste and serve with white truffle shavings, if using.

Torta di Spinaci

Spinach Pie

PREHEAT OVEN TO 375° F (190° C)
9-INCH (23 CM) PIE PLATE

SERVES 4 TO 6

A very old, very traditional dish, this makes a delightful light lunch or, served with hearty vegetable soup, a filling supper. If you're not keen on making your own pastry, rolled out sheets of commercial frozen puff pastry can be used to make the pie, just remember to increase the oven temperature accordingly.

1 lb	rich pastry (homemade or store-bought)	500 g
2 1/2 lbs	fresh spinach	1.25 kg
3 tbsp	golden raisins	45 mL
8 oz	ricotta	250 g
3/4 cup	grated Pecorino Romano	175 mL
2 tbsp	pine nuts	25 mL
Pinch	freshly grated nutmeg	Pinch
	Salt and freshly ground black pepper	
2	eggs, lightly beaten	2
	Milk for brushing pastry	

1. Roll out pastry for the bottom and top of the pie. Line pie plate with one of the pieces of pastry. Keep the other covered with a damp cloth.

2. Trim and wash spinach. Put the spinach in a large saucepan with just the water that clings to the leaves after washing. Cook, covered, over high heat until steam begins to escape from beneath lid. Remove lid, toss spinach and cook 1 minute longer or until tender. Remove from heat. Drain, pressing spinach against sides of colander to squeeze out as much water as possible. Cool. Chop spinach roughly.

3. Soak raisins in hot water; drain and dry. In a large bowl, stir together spinach, ricotta, Pecorino Romano, raisins, pine nuts and nutmeg. Season to taste with salt and pepper. Stir in eggs.

4. Pour filling into pastry shell, spreading it evenly. Top with remaining pastry; trim and flute edges. Brush with milk. Bake 40 to 50 minutes or until pastry is golden. Let stand 5 minutes before serving.

MAKES ABOUT 12

In the Puglian town of Lecce, my first taste of local cuisine was rustici – a rather odd name, I thought, for such delightfully refined little pastries. And while I enjoyed many more rustici thereafter, it was that first one I remember as being the most splendid, chosen as it was from a wonderful array of pastries at a small bakery-cum-espresso-bar. Perhaps it was so magical because I had no idea what I was about to taste. Warm from the oven, the golden parcel of pastry held a hidden creamy cheese filling and a little heart of fresh tomato. "Perfetto!" I announced to the beaming baker, who watched me devour one after another.

Rustici are also called sfogliatine (stuffed pastries) which, when made at home, use various fillings that include bits of leftover meat and vegetables, last bits of cheese, salami, olives – even ragu sauce from the previous day's supper. You can make them large or small, in round, square or oval shapes.

You can make your own recipe for puff pastry if you wish, but I have had excellent results with this recipe using store-bought frozen puff pastry.

Freeze remaining cheese sauce or use in lasagna. Or, thin it down with extra milk and toss it with cooked macaroni for a fast macaroni and cheese dinner.

Rustici

Stuffed Puff Pastries

PREHEAT OVEN TO 400° F (200° C)
TWO BAKING SHEETS, GREASED

6 tbsp	butter	90 mL
2/3 cup	all-purpose flour	150 mL
2 1/3 cups	milk	575 mL
1 1/2 cups	grated Pecorino Romano	375 mL
1 1/2 cups	shredded mozzarella	375 mL
	Salt and freshly ground black pepper	
1 1/2 lbs	puff pastry	750 g
1	egg	1
2	tomatoes (fresh or canned, drained), peeled, seeded and chopped	2

1. In a heavy saucepan, melt butter over low heat. Whisk in flour; cook, stirring constantly, for 5 minutes. Gradually whisk in milk. Increase heat to medium; cook, stirring constantly, for 5 minutes or until thickened and smooth. Stir in cheeses until melted. Season to taste with salt and pepper. Cool to room temperature.

2. On a lightly floured surface, roll puff pastry to 1/8-inch (3 mm) thickness. Using a round 3 1/2-inch (9 cm) cookie cutter, cut out as many circles as possible. Gather up scraps; re-roll and cut into circles. In a small bowl, beat egg with 1 tbsp (15 mL) water; brush egg wash over half of the puff pastry circles and put on prepared baking sheets.

3. Spoon 2 tsp (10 mL) of the cheese sauce in the center of each egg-washed pastry circle; top with a piece of tomato. Top each with one of remaining pastry circles, pressing edges together to seal. Brush tops with remaining egg wash.

4. Bake for 15 minutes. Reduce heat to 350° F (180° C); bake 10 minutes longer or until puffed and golden brown. Serve warm or at room temperature.

ZUPPA
SOUPS

SERVES 6

If you can find them, use the small brown Italian lentils from Umbria or the dark green puy lentils – they don't break up during cooking, and they will nicely absorb any aromatics cooked with them, yet retain their attractive shape. Health food markets are good sources for a wide range of quality pulses, including organic varieties.

Zuppa di Lenticchie

Lentil Soup with Rice

1 tbsp	butter	15 mL
1 tbsp	olive oil	15 mL
2	cloves garlic, finely chopped	2
1	small onion, finely chopped	1
1	stalk celery, finely chopped	1
1	small carrot, finely chopped	1
4 oz	pancetta, finely chopped	125 g
2 tbsp	finely chopped fresh marjoram	25 mL
1 1/2 cups	lentils, rinsed and drained	375 mL
1 1/2 cups	canned plum tomatoes with juices, finely chopped	375 mL
6 cups	beef stock	1.5 L
1/2 cup	short-grained Italian Arborio rice	125 mL
	Salt and freshly ground black pepper to taste	
1/2 cup	grated Parmigiano-Reggiano	125 mL
2 tbsp	chopped celery leaves	25 mL

1. In a saucepan with a lid, melt butter with olive oil over medium heat. Add garlic, onion, celery, carrot, pancetta and marjoram; sauté 5 minutes or until vegetables have softened.

2. Stir in lentils and tomatoes; cook 3 minutes longer. Add beef stock and bring to a boil. Reduce heat to low, cover and cook for 30 minutes or until lentils are almost tender.

3. Stir in rice, replace cover and simmer, stirring occasionally, for another 20 minutes or until rice and lentils are tender. Season to taste with salt and pepper.

4. Serve sprinkled with Parmigiano-Reggiano and celery leaves.

In Friuli, celery soup is traditionally enjoyed on Christmas Eve and, certainly, this hearty soup is particularly well suited to the winter months.

Using strong beef stock results in a rich-colored, surprisingly dark soup. Use chicken stock (perhaps with a touch of cream) to achieve a celery soup with a lighter hue.

Zuppa di Sedano

Celery Soup

1/4 cup	olive oil	50 mL
1	onion, chopped	1
3 oz	pancetta, finely chopped	75 g
1	head celery, trimmed and diced	1
2 tbsp	tomato paste	25 mL
10 cups	hot beef stock	2.5 L
3/4 cup	short-grained Italian Arborio rice	175 mL
	Salt and freshly ground black pepper to taste	
	Grated Parmigiano-Reggiano	

1. In a large, heavy-bottomed saucepan with a lid, heat oil over medium heat. Add onion and pancetta; cook for 5 minutes or until onion is softened. Stir in celery and tomato paste; cook 10 minutes longer, stirring occasionally.

2. Stir in stock and bring to a boil. Reduce heat to medium-low, cover and simmer for 20 minutes. Stir in rice; cook, covered, 15 minutes longer or until rice is just cooked through. Season to taste with salt and pepper. Serve sprinkled with Parmigiano-Reggiano.

SERVES 4 TO 6

With its deceivingly bland-sounding name, you might not imagine that this soup has much to offer. But this combination of fresh tomatoes, chilies and good Calabrian-style bread is rustic Italian eating at its best.

If you can find one, use a dark Calabrese loaf for this soup. Of substantial size and weight, this earthy type of bread is almost always baked up big and round – just as they have done for centuries in Calabria. They still make their bread this way and often a family will purchase a loaf of such heft that it lasts them for the whole week. Towards the end of the week the last of the loaf would probably be used to make a soup such as this – hearty, dense and sustaining.

Pane Cotto

Bread Soup

1/4 cup	olive oil	50 mL
2	cloves garlic, finely chopped	2
1	dried chili pepper, broken in half	1
1 lb	ripe plum tomatoes, seeded and chopped *or* canned plum tomatoes, drained, seeded	500 g
3	sprigs flat-leaf parsley, chopped	3
2	bay leaves	2
6 cups	vegetable stock *or* chicken stock	1.5 L
	Salt and freshly ground black pepper	
12	slices rustic Calabrese-style bread, a few days old or oven-toasted	12
	Grated Parmigiano-Reggiano	
	Extra virgin olive oil	

1. In a large, heavy stockpot, heat oil over medium-low heat. Add garlic and chili; cook for 3 minutes or until garlic is softened but not browned.

2. Stir in tomatoes, parsley and bay leaves; cook for 15 minutes, breaking up the tomatoes as they cook.

3. In another saucepan, bring stock to a boil. Stir into tomato mixture; cook 15 minutes longer.

4. Strain the soup, discarding solids. Return soup to stockpot; season to taste with salt and pepper. Tear bread into rough chunks; stir into soup and let stand 3 minutes. Serve immediately, sprinkled with Parmigiano-Reggiano and drizzled with extra virgin olive oil.

This great big cold-weather soup is a favorite in the north-eastern regions of Trentino and Friuli.

Zuppa d'Orzo alla Trentina

Barley Soup Trentino

4 cups	beef stock	1 L
1/2 cup	pearl barley, rinsed and drained	125 mL
2 tbsp	olive oil	25 mL
1	onion, finely chopped	1
1	carrot, finely chopped	1
1	stalk celery, finely chopped	1
3 oz	prosciutto, finely chopped	75 g
1 tsp	finely chopped rosemary	5 mL
1 tsp	finely chopped flat-leaf parsley	5 mL
1	large boiling potato, peeled and chopped	1
	Salt and freshly ground black pepper to taste	
	Grated Parmigiano-Reggiano	

1. In a large saucepan with a lid, combine beef stock and barley. Bring to a boil; reduce heat to low and cook, partially covered, for 45 minutes or until barley is tender.

2. In a skillet heat olive oil over medium heat. Add onion, carrot, celery, prosciutto, rosemary, parsley and potato; cook for 5 minutes or until vegetables are softened. Stir into barley and beef stock. Bring to a boil; reduce heat to low and cook 30 minutes or until potato is tender and soup is thick. Season to taste with salt and pepper. Serve sprinkled with Parmigiano-Reggiano.

Pasta e Ceci

Pappardelle and Chickpea Soup

SERVES 6 TO 8

Pappardelle are long, ribbon-like strips of pasta, about 3/4 inch (2 cm) in width. They are often used with rich, creamy sauces, with porcini and, famously, with rabbit. (See recipe, page 66.) This ancient version pairs the pasta with chickpeas as they do in Apulia where, just before serving, they often fry a little additional dried pasta at the very last minute to add another dimension of texture to the soup.

It's worth taking the time to use dried chickpeas and soak them overnight. Canned chickpeas are often overcooked.

The rosemary is not traditional but works well with the chickpeas.

If using smaller canned plum tomatoes, add 2 to 3 more.

2 cups	dried chickpeas, soaked overnight in cold water to cover	500 mL
1	bay leaf	1
3 cups	vegetable stock *or* chicken stock	750 mL
1/4 cup	olive oil	50 mL
1	onion, chopped	1
3	cloves garlic, finely chopped	3
1	whole branch rosemary	1
3	large ripe plum tomatoes, peeled, seeded and chopped	3
	Salt and freshly ground black pepper to taste	
8 oz	*pappardelle* (or tagliatelle or fettucine)	250 g
1/2 cup	chopped flat-leaf parsley	125 mL

1. In a large saucepan, combine drained chickpeas and bay leaf; add cold water to cover by 2 inches (5 cm). Bring to a boil; reduce heat to simmer and cook 1 hour or until chickpeas are tender. Drain, reserving cooking liquid. Wipe saucepan clean and return cooking liquid to saucepan. Add stock; bring to a boil and reduce heat to low.

2. In another large saucepan, heat olive oil over medium heat. Add onion, garlic and rosemary; cook for 5 minutes or until vegetables are softened. Stir in tomatoes; cook 5 minutes longer. Stir in stock mixture and chickpeas. Season to taste with salt and pepper. Bring to a boil; stir in pasta, reduce heat to simmer and cook, stirring occasionally, for 10 minutes or until pasta is tender.

3. Remove rosemary. Serve sprinkled with parsley.

A cross between a soup and a pasta dish, I reserve this vibrantly colored zuppa for the late summer months, when plum tomatoes are plentiful. The most cooking-challenged novice can easily make this soup.

Ditalini are small, short pasta tubes that are made especially for soup. They lend a wonderful texture to this simple preparation, but if you cannot locate any, use your favorite short, hollow pasta.

Peeling fresh tomatoes may sound a tedious chore, but it is effortless if you follow this method: Plunge firm tomatoes into a large pot of boiling water for 2 minutes and remove with a slotted spoon to a bowl of cold water; after a few minutes, the tomato skins should be easy to remove with a sharp paring knife. Alternatively, use a good quality, broad-bladed vegetable peeler to remove skins from fresh tomatoes.

Zuppa del Contadino

Peasant Soup

3 tbsp	olive oil	45 mL
3	garlic cloves, finely chopped	3
1	onion, peeled and chopped	1
1 lb	plum tomatoes (ripe but firm), peeled and chopped	500 g
8 cups	chicken stock	2 L
	Salt and freshly ground black pepper to taste	
12 oz	*ditalini*	375 g
6	slices rustic country-style bread, brushed with olive oil and grilled or oven-toasted	6
1/4 cup	roughly chopped flat-leaf parsley	50 mL

1. In a large saucepan, heat olive oil over medium heat. Add garlic and onion; cook for 5 minutes or until softened. Stir in tomatoes and stock. Season to taste with salt and pepper.

2. Bring to a boil. Stir in pasta, reduce heat to simmer and cook 10 minutes or until pasta is tender.

3. Put a piece of toasted bread in the bottom of each soup plate. Ladle soup over toast. Sprinkle with parsley; serve immediately.

A long-time favorite soup, pasta fagioli combines beans, pasta and vegetables to make a delicious meal-in-a-bowl. Italian-born Toronto chef Massimo Capra, of Mistura Restaurant, makes a version that uses different types of beans. The actual combination of beans can be varied to suit your taste and may either be canned, dried, fresh or frozen. If using canned beans, rinse and drain well.

One day I was wondering what to do with leftovers of this soup and some soft polenta. So I shaped the polenta into small patties, fried them in a little butter, placed them in the bottom of a shallow soup plate and poured the hot soup over to cover slightly. Ambrosial!

Pasta Fagioli Capra

Bean and Pasta Soup Capra

3 tbsp	extra virgin olive oil	45 mL
1	stalk celery, finely chopped	1
1	small onion, finely chopped	1
1	small carrot, finely chopped	1
6	cloves garlic, finely chopped	6
1	sprig thyme, leaves only, finely chopped	1
2	bay leaves	2
1 cup	chopped plum tomatoes, canned or fresh	250 mL
1/4 cup	cooked romano beans	50 mL
1/4 cup	cooked black-eyed peas	50 mL
1/4 cup	cooked *cannellini* beans (white kidney beans) *or* navy beans	50 mL
1/4 cup	cooked large lima beans	50 mL
1/4 cup	cooked chickpeas	50 mL
6 cups	vegetable stock	1.5 L
	Salt and freshly ground black pepper	
	Freshly grated nutmeg	
1 cup	*maccheroni* (the straight, short variety) *or* ditalini *or* tubetti	250 mL
1/2 cup	cooked, peeled fava beans	125 mL
1/4 cup	roughly chopped flat-leaf parsley	50 mL
	Olive oil	
6	slices of rustic country-style bread brushed with olive oil and grilled or oven-toasted	6

1. In a large saucepan, heat olive oil over medium heat. Add celery, onion, carrot, garlic, thyme and bay leaves; cook for 5 minutes or until vegetables are softened. Stir in tomatoes; cook, stirring, for 3 minutes.

2. Stir in romano beans, black-eyed peas, kidney beans, lima beans and chickpeas. Add stock and bring to a boil. Reduce heat to simmer and cook for 15 minutes, skimming any foam that rises to the top. Season to taste with salt, pepper and nutmeg.

3. Stir in pasta and fava beans; return to a simmer and cook, stirring occasionally, 10 minutes or just until pasta is tender.

4. Stir in parsley. Drizzle with olive oil and serve immediately with toasts.

Perhaps no other soup from the Italian cucina is as widely travelled – or so much abused as this one, served up as it so often is with completely over-cooked pasta and vegetables and many, many huge red kidney beans. If your relation-ship with this fine soup has been restricted to the can or the cafeteria, take an afternoon to make a pot of the real thing.

Prepare the Parmigiano-Reggiano toasts while the soup is cooking. Place one on each serving and watch the rest disappear tableside.

It seems that every region of Italy has a version of mine-strone, which literally translates as "big soup." While it often includes Arborio rice, I have omitted it as it makes an already full-bodied soup even thicker.

Reserve white part of leeks for making stock.

Minestrone Toscano

Tuscan Vegetable Soup

BAKING SHEET

Soup

1 1/2 cups	dried *cannellini* beans (white kidney beans) *or* navy beans, soaked overnight in water to cover	375 mL
1/4 cup	olive oil	50 mL
3	cloves garlic, finely chopped	3
2	stalks celery, finely chopped	2
2	branches rosemary, leaves only, finely chopped	2
1	small onion, finely chopped	1
1	carrot, finely chopped	1
6 cups	chicken stock	1.5 L
2 tbsp	tomato paste	25 mL
Half	small head Savoy cabbage, cored and shredded (about 6 cups [1.5 L])	Half
2	leeks, green part only, washed and chopped	2
2	small zucchini, trimmed and finely chopped	2
	Salt and freshly ground black pepper	
12	basil leaves, roughly chopped	12

Toasts

1/2 cup	extra virgin olive oil	125 mL
1	long Italian loaf of rustic country-style bread (or baguette) cut diagonally into 1-inch (2.5 cm) slices	1
1 1/2 cups	ricotta cheese	375 mL
3 cups	grated Parmigiano-Reggiano	750 mL
1/4 cup	chopped flat-leaf parsley	50 mL

1. Make the soup: In a large saucepan, combine drained beans with 6 cups (1.5 L) cold water. Bring to a boil; reduce heat to simmer and cook for 1 hour or until beans are tender. Meanwhile, in a large skillet, heat olive oil over medium heat. Add garlic, celery, rosemary, onion and carrot; cook for 10 minutes or until vegetables are softened.

2. When beans are tender, stir vegetable mixture into beans (do not drain), along with chicken stock, tomato paste and cabbage. Bring to a boil; reduce heat to simmer and cook for 10 minutes. Stir in leeks and zucchini; cook for 15 minutes longer or until vegetables are tender. Meanwhile, make the toasts.

3. Toasts: Preheat oven to 400° F (200° C). In a heavy skillet, heat olive oil over medium-high heat. In batches, cook bread slices for 1 minute per side, or until golden brown. Drain on paper towel.

4. Divide ricotta among toasts; spread over surface. Place on baking sheet. Sprinkle with some of the Parmigiano-Reggiano. Bake for 5 minutes or until cheese is golden. Sprinkle toasts with parsley.

5. Season soup to taste with salt and pepper. Stir in basil. Serve soup with cheese toasts, with remaining Parmigiano-Reggiano on the side.

Hearty bean soups are almost a way of life in Italy – especially in Tuscany, where the residents have long been known as mangia fagioli or "bean eaters." Sustaining, filling and satisfying, these soups (which also include minestrone or pasta fagioli) form the basis of the next day's supper. This is the inspiration for sturdy ribollita, which means "reboiled."

I have made a wonderful ribollita with leftovers from TUSCAN BEANS *(see recipe, page 155) and* TUSCAN MINESTRONE *(see recipe, page 46). A bowl of this thick, rib-sticking soup, a wonderful amalgam of hearty beans (some of which are puréed) with good cheese and bread, will leave you feeling as though you can conquer Rome, or at least rush hour.*

Ribollita

Thick Bean Soup

12-CUP (3 L) SOUP TUREEN OR CASSEROLE DISH

3 tbsp	olive oil	45 mL
3	cloves garlic, finely chopped	3
2	medium leeks, green part only, trimmed, washed and finely chopped	2
1	onion, finely chopped	1
1	carrot, finely chopped	1
1	stalk celery, finely chopped	1
2 tsp	finely chopped rosemary	10 mL
1	small dried chili pepper	1
1 1/4 cups	dried *cannellini* beans (white kidney beans) *or* navy beans, soaked overnight in water to cover	300 mL
	Salt and freshly ground black pepper to taste	
1/2 cup	extra virgin olive oil	125 mL
2	cloves garlic, crushed	2
2	whole sprigs thyme	2
8	slices oven-toasted or grilled bread, brushed with olive oil and rubbed with garlic	8
1 cup	grated Parmigiano-Reggiano	250 mL

1. In a large saucepan, heat olive oil over medium heat. Add garlic, leeks, onion, carrot, celery, rosemary and chili; cook, stirring frequently, for 10 minutes or until vegetables are softened and are starting to brown. Stir in drained beans and 10 cups (2.5 L) water. Bring to a boil; reduce heat to simmer and cook 1 1/2 hours or until beans are tender, skimming any foam that rises to the surface.

2. With a slotted spoon, transfer half of the cooked beans and vegetables to a food processor or blender; purée. Return bean purée to saucepan; stir to blend. Season to taste with salt and pepper. Keep soup at low simmer.

3. Preheat oven to 375° F (190° C). In a small skillet, heat olive oil over medium heat. Add garlic and thyme; cook 2 minutes or until garlic is golden. Strain oil into a heatproof bowl; discard solids.

4. Put toasts in bottom of soup tureen or casserole dish; sprinkle with half of the cheese. Pour bean soup over toasts. Drizzle garlic-thyme oil over the surface. Sprinkle with remaining cheese. Bake uncovered for 30 minutes or until cheese is golden. Serve from tureen at the table.

SERVES 4 TO 6

This may be the best bean soup ever. The cooking time will depend on the freshness of the soaked beans. Health food stores are a good source for high-quality organic beans and pulses. Don't add salt to the beans' cooking water; this toughens them and encourages them to split open.

Zuppa di Fagioli con Biete

White Bean Soup with Swiss Chard

2 cups	dried *cannellini* beans (white kidney beans) *or* navy beans, soaked overnight in water to cover	500 mL
1 tbsp	olive oil	15 mL
8 oz	mushrooms, finely chopped (about 3 cups [750 mL])	250 g
3	cloves garlic, minced	3
1	onion, chopped	1
1/2 tsp	freshly grated nutmeg	2 mL
6 cups	chicken stock	1.5 L
1 lb	Swiss chard, washed, stemmed and chopped (about 6 cups [1.5 L])	500 g
	Salt and freshly ground black pepper to taste	
3 cups	ricotta cheese	750 mL
8	slices rustic country-style bread	8
3/4 cup	grated Pecorino Romano	175 mL
1/4 cup	chopped flat-leaf parsley	50 mL

1. Drain beans and add to a large saucepan. Add water to cover by 2 inches (5 cm). Bring to a boil; reduce heat to simmer and cook 1 1/2 hours or until beans are tender, skimming foam that rises to the surface. Drain beans, discarding cooking liquid.

2. Wipe saucepan clean. Add olive oil to saucepan; heat over medium heat. Add mushrooms, garlic, onion and nutmeg; cook for 5 minutes, stirring often, or until vegetables are softened. Stir in cooked beans and chicken stock. Bring to a boil, reduce heat to medium-low and cook 20 minutes. Stir in Swiss chard; cook 2 minutes or until wilted. Season to taste with salt and pepper.

3. Preheat broiler. Spread ricotta on bread slices. Top with Pecorino Romano. Broil 2 minutes or until cheese is golden.

4. Ladle soup into soup plates. Place a piece of cheese toast in the center of each serving. Sprinkle with parsley. Serve with extra toasts on the side.

SERVES 6

*This creamy soup has few
ingredients but much style and
flavor. The Italians usually
mean butternut squash when
they refer to zucca. Either
pumpkin (the small sugar
pumpkin variety) or butternut
squash may be used in this
recipe.*

*Depending on the region,
Italians either adore or revile
pumpkin and squash. In
Mantua they devote a yearly
festival to it and prepare it
fried, made into soups, or as an
ingredient in rice dishes. In
Parma they use it as a filling in
tortelli and in Ferrara (where
the people are called magnazoca or "pumpkin eaters"), they
make cappellacci, another
type of stuffed pasta. In Friuli
they make light gnocchi with
pumpkin or butternut squash,
creatively flavored with lemon,
nutmeg and brandy.*

Minestra di Zucca e Spaghetti

Pumpkin Soup with Spaghetti

5 cups	milk	1.25 L
1 cup	chicken stock	250 mL
1 lb	piece of pumpkin or butternut squash, peeled, seeded and chopped	500 g
	Salt and freshly ground black pepper to taste	
1 cup	broken spaghetti	250 mL
2 tbsp	butter	25 mL
3/4 cup	grated Parmigiano-Reggiano	175 mL
	Freshly grated nutmeg to taste	

1. In a large saucepan, combine milk and chicken stock. Bring to a boil over medium-high heat. Stir in pumpkin; cook 10 minutes or until pumpkin is tender. With a slotted spoon, transfer pumpkin to a food processor or blender; purée. Return purée to saucepan; stir to blend. Season to taste with salt and pepper.

2. Bring soup to a boil over medium-high heat. Stir in spaghetti; cook for 10 minutes or until pasta is tender but firm. Remove from heat. Stir in butter. Serve sprinkled with Parmigiano-Reggiano and nutmeg.

PASTA & POLENTA

In Italy, pasta and polenta dishes are generally served as a first course and a precursor to what North Americans call a "main course" – usually consisting of meat, poultry or seafood. Therefore the suggested serving is somewhat less than if you choose to feature these dishes as a main course.

SERVES 4 TO 6

*Buy the best quality dried
porcini you can find. Cheaper
varieties have inferior flavor –
and may include extraneous
bits of forest floor fodder!*

Tagliatelle con Porcini

Tagliatelle with Porcini

2 oz	assorted dried porcini, chanterelles, shiitake, hedgehog or morels *or* 1 oz (25 g) dried porcini plus 12 oz (375 g) cremini or fresh white mushrooms	50 g
1/4 cup	olive oil	50 mL
3	cloves garlic, finely chopped	3
2	shallots, finely chopped	2
1/2 cup	dry white wine	125 mL
3/4 cup	chicken stock	175 mL
	Salt and freshly ground black pepper	
1 tsp	coarse salt	5 mL
1 lb	fresh tagliatelle, fettuccine or pappardelle (or 12 oz [375 g] dried)	500 g
3 tbsp	chopped flat-leaf parsley	45 mL
1/2 cup	grated Parmigiano-Reggiano	125 mL

1. In a small bowl, soak dried mushrooms in warm water to cover. (Use only 1 cup [250 mL] warm water if using a combination of dried and fresh mushrooms.) Let stand for 1 hour. Strain through a sieve lined with cheesecloths or coffee filters, reserving liquid. Chop mushrooms finely. Set mushrooms and soaking liquid aside.

2. In a large skillet, heat olive oil over medium-low heat. Add garlic and shallots; cook 2 minutes or until softened. Stir in mushrooms; cook 5 minutes, stirring occasionally. Pour in wine; cook 3 minutes longer. Stir in stock and mushroom soaking liquid; bring to a boil. Reduce heat to medium; cook 12 minutes or until slightly thickened. Season to taste with salt and pepper.

3. Add coarse salt to a large pot of boiling water. Cook pasta until tender but firm; drain. In a large warmed bowl, toss pasta, mushroom sauce and parsley. Serve with Parmigiano-Reggiano.

SERVES 6

My good friend Arpi Magyar, chef and owner of Toronto's Splendido Restaurant and the owner of Cucina, has had splendid ricotta gnocchi on his menu forever. They are sublime, silky little pillows of loveliness, licked with butter, that slip lightly down the throat. If you can't visit Splendido, try this Magyar-inspired recipe. It is very easy to make and very good. Serve the gnocchi with a little drizzled butter (I'll leave the amount up to you!) and grated Parmigiano-Reggiano or with a simple fresh tomato sauce.

It is important to use dry ricotta here, since the more water it contains, the more flour it will absorb – and the heavier your gnocchi will be. Good quality ricotta may need only a little draining. Use your hands to press very wet ricotta against the sides of the sieve to remove as much water as possible.

Gnocchi di Ricotta

Ricotta Gnocchi

1 lb	fresh ricotta	500 g
2	eggs	2
2	egg yolks	2
Pinch	salt	Pinch
1/2 cup	grated Parmigiano-Reggiano	125 mL
1 1/2 cups	all-purpose flour (approximate)	375 mL
	Melted butter	
	Freshly ground black pepper	

1. Place ricotta in a sieve set over a bowl. Let stand for a few minutes if ricotta is quite wet. Discard liquids and wipe bowl clean. In a bowl, using a wooden spoon, stir together drained ricotta, eggs, egg yolks, salt and half of the grated Parmigiano-Reggiano until well-mixed. Stir in 1 cup (250 mL) flour, 1/4 cup (50 mL) at a time. Stir in enough of remaining flour to make a firm but soft dough.

2. Using a 1 tbsp (15 mL) measuring spoon, portion out dough and shape into small dumplings, more oval than round. Place on a large baking sheet lined with waxed paper, spacing them apart so they don't stick to each other.

3. In a large pot of lightly salted boiling water, cook gnocchi in batches of a dozen at a time for 5 minutes or until gnocchi bob to surface of water and are no longer starchy-tasting. Remove with a slotted spoon to a warm serving dish.

4. Drizzle gnocchi with melted butter and sprinkle with remaining cheese and lots of freshly ground black pepper. Serve immediately.

SERVES 6

With all the butter, egg yolks, pancetta and cheese, this is not exactly a dish for the fat-phobic. Still, in the following classic version of this seductive pasta dish, we do forego the usual North American tradition of adding heavy cream. So don't reject it outright. You can always justify the richness of the ingredients with smaller servings.

Make sure the pasta is very hot when combined with the raw eggs. This is the only "cooking" they will receive.

While we usually think of spaghetti as the natural partner in a carbonara combination, I think the sturdier rigatoni makes a more authentic match. My daughter Jenna says that with rigatoni, the lovely bits of bacon have more to cling to and so don't get lost at the bottom of the bowl – and she's right!

Rigatoni alla Carbonara

Rigatoni with Eggs, Bacon and Cheese

2 tbsp	olive oil	25 mL
2 tbsp	butter	25 mL
4 oz	pancetta *or* unsmoked bacon, cut into thin strips	125 g
4	eggs	4
1/4 cup	grated Parmigiano-Reggiano	50 mL
1/4 cup	grated Pecorino Romano	50 mL
3 tbsp	chopped flat-leaf parsley	45 mL
1/4 tsp	salt	1 mL
1/4 tsp	freshly ground black pepper	1 mL
1 tsp	coarse salt	5 mL
1 lb	rigatoni	500 g
	Additional freshly ground black pepper	

1. In a large skillet, heat olive oil and butter over medium heat. Add pancetta and cook for 5 minutes or until slightly brown but not crisp. Set aside. In a large bowl, whisk together eggs, Parmigiano-Reggiano, Pecorino Romano, parsley, salt and pepper. Set aside.

2. Add coarse salt to a large pot of boiling water. Cook rigatoni until tender but firm; drain and return to pot. Turn heat off and return pot to warm burner. Pour egg mixture over cooked pasta, tossing with two forks. Scrape skillet containing pancetta into pot and toss again. Serve immediately, sprinkled with more freshly ground black pepper.

SERVES 6

Here's a Sicilian dish that combines eggplant, fresh tomatoes and basil. In Sicily this dish is known as Pasta alla Norma, named after a Sicilian opera.

Here, as in other recipes, I have opted to brush the eggplant with a little olive oil and oven-roast – rather than pan-fry – to keep it from absorbing too much oil.

Use good quality Pecorino Romano for this recipe.

Spaghetti con Melanzane e Basilico

Spaghetti with Eggplant and Basil

PREHEAT OVEN TO 400° F (200° C)
LARGE NONSTICK BAKING SHEET

1	large eggplant, unpeeled, sliced into 1/2-inch (1 cm) rounds	1
1 tsp	salt	5 mL
1 tbsp	extra virgin olive oil	15 mL
1/4 cup	olive oil	50 mL
3	cloves garlic, roughly chopped	3
1 lb	fresh plum tomatoes, peeled, seeded and roughly chopped *or* 4 cups (1 L) canned Italian plum tomatoes, drained and chopped	500 g
	Freshly ground black pepper	
1 tsp	coarse salt	5 mL
1 lb	spaghetti	500 g
1/4 cup	grated Pecorino Romano	50 mL
16	basil leaves, roughly chopped	16

1. Put sliced eggplant in a colander and set in sink. Sprinkle with 1/2 tsp (2 mL) of the salt. Put a plate over the eggplant and add a weight. Let stand 30 minutes. Pat eggplant slices dry with paper towel. Brush both sides lightly with the extra virgin olive oil. Cut each slice into quarters. Put on baking sheet and bake for 16 minutes, turning once or twice, or until golden and tender.

2. Meanwhile, in a large skillet, heat 1/4 cup (50 mL) olive oil over medium heat. Add garlic and cook for 3 minutes or until softened, but not browned. Stir in tomatoes, remaining 1/2 tsp (2 mL) salt and lots of freshly ground black pepper; reduce heat to medium-low and cook, stirring occasionally, for 20 minutes or until thickened.

3. Add coarse salt to a large pot of boiling water. Cook spaghetti until tender but firm; drain and return to pot. Turn half the cooked pasta into a warmed serving bowl; add half the tomato sauce, half the eggplant and half the grated cheese. Add remaining pasta, tomato sauce, eggplant and cheese; top with basil and toss together gently. Serve immediately.

SERVES 6

Because this dish is so simple, it has nothing to hide behind, which means you absolutely must use the very best extra virgin olive oil and spaghettini.

If you can find them, use the firmer salt-packed anchovies; otherwise, regular canned anchovies will do. In Europe, these meaty little fish are sold in supermarkets packed in small glass jars. So the next time you are overseas, bring home as many as you can carry – they're worth it.

Spaghettini Aglio, Olio e Peperoncino

Spaghettini with Garlic, Olive Oil and Chili

1 tsp	coarse salt	5 mL
1 lb	spaghettini	500 g
1/2 cup	olive oil	125 mL
3	cloves garlic, finely chopped	3
8	salt-packed anchovies, de-boned *or* 16 oil-packed anchovy fillets, rinsed, patted dry and roughly chopped	8
3 tbsp	finely chopped flat-leaf parsley	45 mL
1/4 to 1/2 tsp	red pepper flakes	1 to 2 mL
	Salt and freshly ground black pepper	

1. Bring a large pot of water to a boil. Stir in salt. Cook spaghettini until tender but firm. Meanwhile, make sauce.

2. In a skillet heat olive oil over medium heat. Add garlic and cook for 2 minutes or until softened, but not browned. Stir in anchovies, parsley, red pepper flakes, a pinch of salt and lots of freshly ground black pepper; cook, stirring, for 2 minutes or until anchovies are heated through. Set aside.

3. Drain cooked pasta; return to pot. With a rubber spatula, scrape anchovy mixture onto pasta. Toss to coat. Season to taste with salt and pepper. Serve immediately.

Orecchiette – "little ears" – are the traditional pasta in the southern Italian region of Apulia. There are a number of good commercial brands available; just check cooking times, since they vary from brand to brand.

A few years ago in Lecce, I watched three women make hundreds of orecchiette at a table set up in a sun-flooded piazza. I was amazed at the speed with which their hands flew back and forth, rolling and shaping the dough to form the dainty little cup-shaped pasta that holds sauce so well. They smiled shyly at their own dexterity as they repeated a centuries-old tradition of pasta making.

In Apulia, they follow the method used here of cooking the greens along with the pasta.

Turnip tops, arugula, dandelion greens or any slightly bitter green may be substituted for rapini.

Orecchiette con Cime di Rape

Orecchiette with Rapini

1 lb	rapini (broccoli rabe)	500 g
1/4 cup	olive oil	50 mL
3	large cloves garlic, chopped	3
6	anchovy fillets (salt-packed if available), rinsed, patted dry and chopped	6
1/2 tsp	red pepper flakes (optional)	2 mL
1 tsp	coarse salt	5 mL
1 lb	*orecchiette*	500 g
3 tbsp	grated *ricotta salata* (a hard, salted version of ricotta) *or* Pecorino Romano	45 mL
	Salt and freshly ground black pepper	
	Additional grated Pecorino Romano	

1. Wash rapini. Trim and discard thick stalks. Roughly chop thinner stalks and leaves, keeping the little florets intact. Set aside.

2. In a skillet heat olive oil over medium heat. Add garlic and cook for 2 minutes or until softened. Stir in anchovies, mashing with the back of a spoon until paste-like. Stir in red pepper flakes, if using. Set sauce aside and keep warm.

3. Bring a large pot of water to a boil. Stir in coarse salt and chopped rapini; cook for 3 minutes. Stir in pasta; cook until pasta is tender but firm. Drain; transfer pasta and rapini to a warmed serving bowl. Toss with sauce and grated cheese. Season to taste with salt and pepper. Serve immediately, sprinkled with additional grated cheese, if desired.

SERVES 6

Years ago I lived in a tiny bed-sitter in the north London district of Muswell Hill, where I recall subsisting mostly on risotto, Leicester cheese, Branston pickle and Jacob's Cream Crackers. But once a week, the young Welsh newly-wed who lived down the hall would make her husband's favorite – "spag bol," as they short-form it in England – and occasionally she would invite me in for a taste. At the time I thought it delicious, due in large part, no doubt, to my growling tum.

Many years later in Italy I tasted the real thing and learned that, in fact, the Bolognese would never dream of eating this meaty sauce with spaghetti – preferring tagliatelle, maccheroni, fettuccine or rigatoni. I like it best with long-cut ziti, but would enjoy it just as much simply spooned onto good bread! Use this sauce to make the world's greatest lasagna.

This recipe produces a rich, meaty, almost dry preparation with colorful flecks of carrot and a flavor that can only result from good red wine and a lengthy cooking time. Although some versions of this dish call for the addition of tomatoes, I prefer to use a small amount of good tomato paste.

Ragù Bolognese

Bolognese Sauce

1/4 cup	olive oil	50 mL
2	cloves garlic, finely chopped	2
1	onion, finely diced	1
1	carrot, finely diced	1
2	stalks celery, finely diced	2
12 oz	extra lean ground beef	375 g
12 oz	pork loin, finely chopped *or* lean ground pork	375 g
4 oz	pancetta, finely chopped	125 g
3	plump fresh chicken livers, washed, trimmed and finely chopped	3
Pinch	freshly grated nutmeg	Pinch
1 cup	red wine	250 mL
1 tbsp	tomato paste	15 mL
1/2 tsp	salt	2 mL
1/4 tsp	freshly ground black pepper	1 mL
1 tsp	coarse salt	5 mL
1 lb	tagliatelle, maccheroni *or* fettuccine	500 g
1 cup	grated Parmigiano-Reggiano	250 mL

1. In a large skillet, heat olive oil over medium heat. Add garlic and onion; cook for 3 minutes or until softened. Stir in carrot and celery; cook, stirring occasionally, for 10 minutes or until vegetables are softened.

2. Add beef, pork, pancetta, chicken livers and nutmeg; cook, stirring to break up meat, for 10 minutes or until meat is browned. Stir in red wine. Bring to a boil; cook for 5 minutes. Stir together tomato paste and 1/2 cup (125 mL) warm water; stir into meat mixture. Return to a boil, reduce heat to low and stir in salt and pepper. Cover and cook for 1 1/2 to 2 hours, stirring occasionally, or until meat is very tender. If ragù appears too dry as it cooks, add a little more water or wine.

3. When ragù is almost finished, bring a large pot of
    water to a boil. Stir in coarse salt. Cook pasta until
    tender but firm; drain and transfer to a warmed serv-
    ing bowl. Pour ragù over pasta; toss to coat. Serve
    immediately, sprinkled with Parmigiano-Reggiano.

SERVES 6

I often think the inspiration for this book began when I first tasted this dish. Long before Toronto chef Chris McDonald owned the revered Avalon, he was cooking at a small Italianate trattoria called Massimo's. It was there one frigid, blustery January night that I sat with my daughter at a plain wooden table and tasted my first pizzocheri – nut-brown buckwheat fettuccine cradling boiled potatoes, melting fontina and small wedges of Savoy cabbage. I was absolutely captivated. If ever a dish was made for a Canadian winter, this is it. It is the embodiment of rustic, hearty and sustaining Italian food.

Despite its name, buckwheat – a.k.a. grano saraceno *(the grain of the Saracens) – is not actually wheat. The Moors are responsible for introducing it to Italy in the Middle Ages. At one time it was used for making bread throughout the country. Today there are only two areas where it is grown – the Veneto region where it is used to make polenta, and Lombardy where they use it to make another form of polenta and* pizzocheri.

Pizzoccheri

Buckwheat Pasta with Fontina, Potatoes and Cabbage

12-CUP (3 L) CASSEROLE DISH, BUTTERED
PREHEAT OVEN TO 450° F (230° C)

1 tsp	coarse salt	5 mL
2 or 3	potatoes, peeled, cut into small chunks	2 or 3
8 oz	Savoy cabbage, halved, cored and cut into strips	250 g
1 lb	*pizzoccheri* (available at Italian grocery stores) *or* fettuccine	500 g
3 tbsp	butter	45 mL
6	cloves garlic, thinly sliced	6
12	sage leaves, torn into pieces	12
Pinch	salt	Pinch
Pinch	freshly ground black pepper	Pinch
1 cup	grated Parmigiano-Reggiano	250 mL
10 oz	Italian fontina *or* Taleggio cheese, diced	300 g

1. Bring a large pot of water to a boil. Stir in coarse salt and potatoes. Reduce heat to medium-high; cook for 3 minutes or until potatoes are softened but not cooked through. Stir in cabbage and pasta; increase heat to high and cook for 8 minutes or until pasta is not quite tender but firm. Drain, reserving 1 cup (250 mL) of cooking liquid; return pasta and vegetables to pot. Set aside.

   Recipe continues…

RISOTTO PRIMAVERA • *SPRING RISOTTO* (PAGE 92) ➤
OVERLEAF: RAGÙ BOLOGNESE • *BOLOGNESE SAUCE* (PAGE 62)

2. In a skillet melt butter over medium-low heat. Add garlic, sage, salt and pepper; cook for 3 minutes or until garlic is softened but not browned. Pour mixture over pasta and vegetables, along with all but a heaping tablespoon (15 mL) of the Parmigiano-Reggiano; toss together gently. Put one-third of mixture into prepared casserole dish; top with one-third of diced fontina. Repeat layers twice. Sprinkle with reserved tablespoon (15 mL) Parmigiano-Reggiano. Pour 1/4 cup (50 mL) of reserved cooking liquid over top to moisten slightly.

3. Bake in top half of oven for 7 minutes or until cheese is melted. Let stand for 5 minutes before serving.

≺ OSSO BUCO • *VEAL SHANKS WITH RED WINE SAUCE* (PAGE 108)

SERVES 6

Sugo is Italian for gravy or sauce and, in this recipe, it's a rich, beautifully colored meat sauce that is the perfect accompaniment for wide ribbons of pasta.

In Italy this dish is traditionally made with wild hare or boar. Many supermarkets now sell farm-raised, mild-tasting rabbit that is cleaned and sectioned and ready to cook. If sold whole, ask the butcher to cut the rabbit into pieces for you. This dish is also very good made with venison.

If you can't find pappardelle, look for fresh square pasta sheets (as you would use for lasagna) and cut them into wide 1 1/4-inch (3 cm) strips to imitate pappardelle. Or substitute fettuccine or tagliatelle.

Pappardelle con Sugo di Coniglio

Pappardelle with Rabbit

1/4 cup	olive oil	50 mL
1	small onion, chopped	1
1	carrot, chopped	1
1	stalk celery, chopped	1
3 lbs	rabbit cut into large pieces	1.5 kg
1 1/2 cups	dry red wine	375 mL
2 tbsp	chopped thyme	25 mL
1/2 tsp	salt	2 mL
1/4 tsp	freshly ground black pepper	1 mL
3 tbsp	tomato paste	45 mL
1 tsp	coarse salt	5 mL
1 lb	*pappardelle*	500 g

1. In a large, heavy-bottomed saucepan with a lid, heat olive oil over medium heat. Add onion, carrot and celery; cook for 6 minutes or until softened. Push vegetables to edges of pan and, in batches, brown rabbit pieces in center for about 6 minutes, turning occasionally. Remove rabbit pieces as they are browned.

2. Return all rabbit pieces and their juices to saucepan. Add wine, thyme, salt and pepper. Bring to a boil, scraping any browned bits from bottom of pan; boil for 5 minutes. Reduce heat to medium-low, cover and cook for 1 1/2 hours or until rabbit is very tender and meat pulls easily away from the bone. Remove sauce from heat. Transfer rabbit pieces to a bowl to cool slightly.

3. When cool enough to handle, remove and discard
    bones; pull meat apart or roughly chop and set aside.
    Reheat sauce over medium heat. Whisk in tomato paste
    and bring to a boil. Stir in rabbit meat, reduce heat to
    medium-low and cook, uncovered, for 15 minutes.

4. Meanwhile, bring a large pot of water to a boil. Stir
    in coarse salt. Cook pasta until tender but firm;
    drain. Portion pasta onto serving plates; top with a
    ladleful of sauce. Serve immediately.

While we in North America usually think of gnocchi as miniature dumplings, this recipe uses the term a little more loosely. Here, polenta is cooked and poured out onto a cool surface to set. Then, using the rim of a glass or a cookie cutter, rounds of set polenta are cut out and laid, overlapping one another like roof tiles, in a gratin dish to be baked with a little melted butter, cheese and fresh sage. Alternatively, once the polenta is cooked and cooled slightly, you can make small gnocchi by scooping out egg-shaped portions with a large spoon and proceeding as above.

Enjoy this dish with grilled sausages or pan-seared shrimp or scallops. For a variation, try it with your best tomato or meat sauce recipe and grated Parmigiano-Reggiano. It's also delicious layered with spinach and ricotta cheese.

I have tried both regular and instant polenta with this recipe – both with excellent results.

Gnocchi di Polenta alla Salvia

Polenta Gnocchi with Sage

3 cups	milk *or* half water, half milk	750 mL
1 tsp	coarse salt	5 mL
3 tbsp	butter	45 mL
1 cup	Italian polenta	250 mL
1 cup	grated Parmigiano-Reggiano	250 mL
	Salt and freshly ground (preferably white) pepper	
20	whole sage leaves	20

1. In a large heavy-bottomed saucepan, bring milk to a boil over medium-high heat. Stir in salt and 1 tbsp (15 mL) of the butter. Reduce heat to low; add polenta in a slow, thin stream, whisking constantly. With a wooden spoon, stir every minute or so until the mixture pulls away from the sides of the pan in one mass. (Depending on coarseness of polenta, this will take from 5 to 20 minutes.) Remove from heat; stir in 1/4 cup (50 mL) of Parmigiano-Reggiano. Season to taste with salt and pepper. Pour polenta onto baking sheet; with a metal spatula, spread it out evenly to 1/4-inch (5 mm) thickness. Cover with a clean tea towel. Let stand 30 minutes.

2. Preheat oven to 425° F (220° C). In a small saucepan, combine remaining butter with 12 of the sage leaves; cook over medium heat just until butter is melted. Set aside. With a small cookie cutter or rim of a glass, cut the set polenta into circles. Scatter the end bits of polenta over bottom of prepared casserole dish; drizzle with a little sage butter and sprinkle with a little Parmigiano-Reggiano. Layer polenta circles, overlapping them slightly, and drizzling with remaining sage butter and Parmigiano-Reggiano.

3. Bake uncovered for 20 minutes or until golden. Put remaining sage leaves across the surface, pressing them into the gnocchi slightly. Serve immediately.

SERVES 6

Named for the two colors of pasta – yolk yellow and grass green – that are used in it, this is a rich, sumptuous and elegant dish. Try it as a luxurious first course for a special dinner party.

Tagliolini – thin ribbon noodles – are the best for this dish. If you wish, you can embellish this recipe with slivers of prosciutto, finely sliced mushrooms or a few bright green peas. But at least once, try it just on its own.

Paglia e Fieno

Straw and Hay

1 tsp	coarse salt	5 mL
8 oz	*tagliolini* or other long thin pasta	250 g
8 oz	spinach *tagliolini* or other long thin pasta	250 g
1/4 cup	butter	50 mL
1	onion, finely chopped	1
1	clove garlic, finely chopped	1
1 cup	whipping (35%) cream	250 mL
3/4 cup	grated Parmigiano-Reggiano	175 mL
	Salt and freshly ground black pepper	

1. Bring a large pot of water to a boil. Stir in coarse salt. Cook plain and spinach pastas until tender but firm. Meanwhile, make the sauce.

2. In a large skillet, melt butter over medium-high heat. Add onion and garlic; cook for 3 minutes or until softened. Stir in cream; cook, stirring, for 2 minutes or until bubbling and slightly reduced. Remove from heat.

3. Drain pasta; add to skillet along with Parmigiano-Reggiano. Toss gently. Season to taste with salt and pepper.

Polenta is often considered the definitive rustic peasant staple. But I have to admit that I've never felt particularly peasant-like when I enjoyed this delight-fully rich version. If you're watching your fat intake you can omit the heavy cream, but it does add a wonderful dimen-sion to the finished dish. I pre-fer the fine-grain variety of instant polenta for this recipe.

This is lovely with grilled or stewed meat dishes.

Polentina con Fonduta

Polenta with Fontina

2 cups	milk	500 mL
1 tbsp	unsalted butter	15 mL
1 tbsp	coarse salt	15 mL
1 1/2 cups	Italian polenta	375 mL
8 oz	Italian fontina cheese, shredded	250 g
2 cups	grated Parmigiano-Reggiano	500 mL
1 cup	whipping (35%) cream	250 mL

1. In a large heavy-bottomed saucepan, bring milk and 2 cups (500 mL) water to a boil over medium-high heat. Stir in butter and salt. Reduce heat to low; add polenta in a slow, thin stream, whisking constantly. With a wooden spoon, stir every minute or so until the mixture pulls away from the sides of the pan in one mass. (Depending on coarseness of polenta, this will take from 5 to 20 minutes.)

2. Stir in fontina and Parmigiano-Reggiano; continue to cook, stirring, until cheese is incorporated. Stir in cream; cook, stirring, until mixture is heated through and smooth. Serve immediately.

Polenta e Baccalà

Polenta and Salt Cod

SERVES 6

Some Italian cooks like to partner cooked salt cod with polenta that has a soft and creamy consistency. But I prefer this combination with polenta that has been set, cut into squares and grilled or pan-fried until slightly crisp. If you opt for the latter version, choose a coarser-grained polenta. Then, follow the procedure for making set polenta in GNOCCHI DI POLENTA ALLA SALVIA (see recipe, page 68). Given the preparation time required, you will need to plan to make this dish a few days in advance.

Salt cod can be tough, so it doesn't hurt to give it a gentle pounding with a kitchen mallet before soaking. When purchasing salt cod, try to get a center cut of the fish.

1 lb	dried salt cod, cut into 3 or 4 pieces	500 g
1/4 cup	fresh lemon juice	50 mL
1/4 cup	extra virgin olive oil	50 mL
3 tbsp	red wine vinegar	45 mL
1	onion, very finely chopped	1
3	cloves garlic, minced	3
1/3 cup	finely chopped flat-leaf parsley	75 mL
1/3 cup	finely chopped mint	75 mL
1 tbsp	finely chopped capers	15 mL
	Freshly ground black pepper to taste	
3 tbsp	olive oil	45 mL
6 to 8	firm Italian polenta squares	6 to 8
	Sprigs flat-leaf parsley	

1. Place salt cod in a large bowl; add cold water to cover. Let soak at room temperature for 36 to 48 hours, changing water every 8 hours. Drain; cut into smaller pieces.

2. Bring a large pot of water to a boil. Stir in lemon juice and salt cod; reduce heat to medium-low and cook for 25 minutes. Drain cod; discard skin and bones. Put in a bowl; with a fork, flake the cod.

3. In a small bowl, whisk together extra virgin olive oil, vinegar, onion, garlic, parsley, mint, capers and pepper to taste. Pour over cod. Using two forks, toss cod with vinaigrette. Let stand 20 minutes to develop flavors.

4. In a nonstick skillet, heat olive oil over medium heat; in batches, cook polenta squares 3 minutes per side or until golden and crispy, transferring to serving platter as they are cooked. Evenly distribute cod mixture over polenta squares. Serve immediately, garnished with parsley.

SERVES 4 TO 6

Buy walnuts in the shell for this dish, since they will always be fresher than packaged walnuts. Because the odd nut in the shell may be shriveled or stale, purchase more than you need – in this case, about 1 lb (500 g) of walnuts, which is a bit more than required.

Tortellini con la Salsa di Noci

Tortellini with Walnut Sauce

1 1/2 cups	fresh shelled walnuts	375 mL
1	thick slice homestyle white bread, crusts trimmed	1
1/4 cup	milk	50 mL
1 tsp	coarse salt	5 mL
1 lb	cheese tortellini	500 g
2	cloves garlic, minced	2
1 tbsp	chopped fresh marjoram	15 mL
3 tbsp	extra virgin olive oil	45 mL
	Salt and freshly ground black pepper	
3 tbsp	butter	45 mL
1/3 cup	mascarpone cheese	75 mL
1/2 cup	grated Parmigiano-Reggiano	125 mL

1. In a large pot of boiling water, blanch walnuts for 2 minutes. Drain and rub skins off. In a skillet set over medium heat, toast walnuts, shaking the pan frequently for 5 minutes or until golden and fragrant. Cool. Put in food processor; pulse on and off until finely powdered. Set aside.

2. In a small bowl, combine bread and milk; let stand for 5 minutes. Drain, discarding milk. Squeeze bread dry with your hands. Set aside.

3. Bring a large pot of water to a boil. Stir in salt. Cook tortellini until tender but firm. Drain, reserving 1 cup (250 mL) of pasta water. Keep tortellini hot in a warmed serving bowl.

4. In a bowl using a fork, combine bread with chopped walnuts. Blend in garlic, marjoram and olive oil. Stir in 3 tbsp (45 mL) of the pasta cooking water or enough to achieve a creamy consistency. Season to taste with salt and pepper.

5. In a small saucepan, melt the butter over medium
    heat. Add mascarpone cheese and cook, stirring
    constantly, for 2 minutes or until smooth and
    creamy. Add to hot tortellini along with hot walnut
    mixture; with two forks, toss together. Add
    Parmigiano-Reggiano, toss together and serve
    immediately.

As Sicilian as Palermo itself, this colorful dish combines cauliflower florets with maccheroni. The quintessentially Sicilian additions of raisins, pine nuts and anchovies combine to produce a vibrant amalgam of colors, tastes and textures.

Use the green-hued variety of cauliflower, if you can find it, and the short tubular macaroni called ditali.

Maccheroni ai Cavolfiori

Pasta with Cauliflower

1 tsp	coarse salt	5 mL
1	large cauliflower, green or white, cleaned, trimmed and left whole	1
1/3 cup	olive oil	75 mL
3	cloves garlic, finely chopped	3
1	medium red onion, thinly sliced	1
4	whole salt-packed anchovies, rinsed and patted dry, bones removed, *or* 8 anchovy fillets, rinsed and patted dry, roughly chopped	4
3 tbsp	tomato paste	45 mL
	Salt and freshly ground black pepper	
1/4 cup	golden raisins	50 mL
1/4 cup	pine nuts	50 mL
1 lb	*ditali* or other short tubular pasta	500 g
1/2 cup	grated Pecorino Romano	125 mL
2 tbsp	chopped flat-leaf parsley	25 mL

1. Bring a large pot of water to a boil. Stir in coarse salt. Place whole cauliflower in boiling water and cook for 10 minutes. With a large slotted spoon, transfer cauliflower to a colander; rinse under cold running water. When cool enough to handle, pull off florets, pat dry and set aside.

2. In a large skillet, heat olive oil over medium heat. Add garlic, onion and anchovies; cook, mashing the anchovies slightly with the back of a fork, for 5 minutes or until onion is softened. Dilute tomato paste in 1/4 cup (50 mL) hot water; stir into skillet. Season to taste with salt and pepper. Reduce heat to low and cook for 10 minutes.

3. Stir cauliflower into sauce; cook, stirring, for 5 minutes or until cauliflower is tender and coated with sauce. Stir in raisins and pine nuts. Keep sauce warm.

4. Return pot of water to the boil. Cook pasta until tender but firm; drain and return to pot. With a rubber spatula, scrape cauliflower sauce onto pasta; toss to coat. Stir in Pecorino Romano and parsley. Season to taste with salt and pepper. Serve immediately.

SERVES 6

Slightly heavier than fettuccine, but about the same width, trenette are flat, narrow noodles that are typically served with pesto. In this dish, featuring the classic Ligurian sauce – based on fresh basil and the finest olive oil – trenette are tossed with new potatoes and pesto. Order this dish in Genoa and it will almost always include young green beans.

While you can make the pesto with a food processor or blender, try using a mortar and pestle. It's a little more work but you will be rewarded with a more authentically textured pesto – and an incredible fragrance in the process. If using this method, make sure that you press the basil leaves against the sides of the mortar to break them down (rather than banging the pestle down directly on them).

Trenette con Pesto e Patate

Trenette with Pesto and Potato

Pesto

1 cup	tightly packed basil leaves, washed and dried	250 mL
1/4 cup	pine nuts *or* fresh shelled walnuts, lightly toasted	50 mL
1/4 cup	grated Pecorino Romano	50 mL
1/4 cup	grated Parmigiano-Reggiano	50 mL
2 or 3	cloves garlic, cut in half	2 or 3
Large pinch	coarse salt	Large pinch
1/2 cup	extra virgin olive oil	125 mL
1 tsp	coarse salt	5 mL
4	new potatoes, peeled and diced	4
1 lb	*trenette* or fettuccine or linguine or tagliatelle	500 g
	Grated Parmigiano-Reggiano	

1. Pesto: In a food processor or blender, combine basil, pine nuts, Pecorino Romano, Parmigiano-Reggiano, garlic, salt and olive oil; purée until smooth. (Alternatively, using a mortar and pestle, pound together basil, pine nuts, garlic and salt to form a paste, stir in cheeses and transfer to a bowl; gradually whisk in olive oil until creamy and smooth.) Set pesto aside. (Pesto can be made up to 2 days in advance; store covered in refrigerator and bring to room temperature before serving.)

2. Bring a large pot of water to a boil. Stir in coarse salt and potatoes; cook for 8 minutes or until potatoes are tender. With a slotted spoon, transfer potatoes to a small bowl and keep warm. Bring water back to the boil. Add pasta and cook until tender but firm; drain, reserving a bit of the cooking water.

3. In a large warmed serving bowl, toss together pasta and potatoes. Stir 3 tbsp (45 mL) pasta cooking water into pesto to thin it slightly. Pour pesto over pasta and potatoes; toss until coated. Serve immediately, sprinkled with grated Parmigiano-Reggiano.

SERVES 6 TO 8

My friend Michael Morelli's family own Ristorante Paradiso in Caserta, Italy where his mum, Amelia D'Agostino, serves up wonderful dishes that are indigenous to the area. When Amelia learned about this cookbook, she very kindly sent along some recipes, and Michael acted as my official translator. Don't be intimidated by the lengthy list of ingredients – the dish is not difficult to prepare and it makes an outstanding first course.

The less you handle gnocchi, the lighter they will be. Less handling also means less flour will be absorbed – another important factor in their lightness and tenderness. If you don't have a food processor or food mill to blend the spinach and potatoes, mix together with your hands.

Gnocchi Paradiso

Spinach and Potato Dumplings

13- BY 9-INCH (3 L) BAKING DISH

Tomato sauce

1/4 cup	olive oil	50 mL
1	large onion, chopped	1
4 cups	ground or puréed tomatoes	1 L
2 cups	canned Italian plum tomatoes, drained and roughly chopped	500 mL
1 tsp	granulated sugar	5 mL
	Salt and freshly ground black pepper	

Meatballs

10 oz	lean ground beef	300 g
3	cloves garlic, minced	3
1/4 cup	chopped flat-leaf parsley	50 mL
1/4 tsp	salt	1 mL
1/4 tsp	freshly ground black pepper	1 mL
2 tbsp	olive oil	25 mL

Gnocchi

1 1/2 lbs	fresh spinach	750 g
1 1/2 lbs	boiling potatoes, scrubbed and halved	750 g
2 1/2 cups	unbleached all-purpose flour (approximate)	625 mL
2	eggs	2
1 tsp	coarse salt	5 mL
1 1/2 to 2 cups	ricotta cheese	375 to 500 mL
1 lb	mozzarella cheese, shredded	500 g

1. Tomato sauce: In a saucepan or large skillet, heat olive oil over medium heat. Add onion and cook for 5 minutes or until softened. Stir in ground and chopped tomatoes and sugar; reduce heat to medium-low and cook for 20 minutes, stirring occasionally. Season to taste with salt and pepper. Distribute sauce evenly over bottom of baking dish; set aside.

2. Meatballs: In a bowl combine ground beef, garlic, parsley, salt and pepper. Shape 1 tsp (5 mL) of mixture into a tiny meatball; repeat until all mixture is used. In a skillet heat olive oil over medium-high heat. In batches, brown the meatballs, shaking the pan from time to time, for 3 minutes or until golden on all sides. With a slotted spoon, transfer to a paper towel-lined plate. Set aside.

3. Gnocchi: Trim and wash spinach. Put spinach in a large saucepan with just the water that clings to the leaves after washing. Cook, covered, over high heat until steam begins to escape from beneath lid. Remove lid, toss spinach and cook 1 minute longer or until tender. Drain, pressing against sides of colander to squeeze out as much water as possible. Cool slightly. Chop finely; set aside.

4. Place potatoes in a large saucepan; add lightly salted cold water to cover. Bring to a boil, reduce heat and simmer until potatoes are tender. Drain and return to pot. Reduce heat and cook, shaking pan occasionally, for 1 minute or until surface moisture is evaporated. When cool enough to handle, remove skins and mash potatoes.

Recipe continues on page 80

5. In a food processor, combine potatoes and spinach; pulse on and off just until blended. (Alternatively, stir together by hand in a large bowl, or put through a food mill until blended.) Turn mixture out onto a clean work surface.

6. Using your hands, gently work in about 1/2 cup (125 mL) of the flour. Work in 1 of the eggs, then another 1/2 cup (125 mL) flour. Work in remaining egg, followed by 1/2 cup (125 mL) flour. Work in just enough of the remaining flour to keep the dough from sticking. Try not to knead the gnocchi dough longer than a few minutes. When dough is smooth, divide into three parts.

7. On a lightly floured board, using your hands, roll each piece of dough into a sausage shape, about 3/4 inch (1 cm) long; transfer to a baking sheet lined with waxed paper, spacing well apart so they don't stick to each other. (Gnocchi can be made to this point several hours ahead of time; cover with plastic wrap and store in refrigerator.)

8. Preheat oven to 350° F (180° C). Add coarse salt to a pot of boiling water. In batches of 20, cook gnocchi for 4 minutes or until they are cooked through and are no longer starchy-tasting. With a slotted spoon, remove to a large bowl. Add meatballs, ricotta and mozzarella to cooked gnocchi; toss gently together. Pour mixture over tomato sauce in the baking dish.

9. Bake for 20 minutes or until heated through and starting to brown slightly. Serve immediately.

RISOTTO
RICE

Risotto al Radicchio e Gorgonzola • *Rice with Radicchio and Gorgonzola* 84

Risotto alla Milanese • *Saffron Risotto* 86

Risotto Rosso di Barbabietola • *Red Beet Risotto* 88

Risotto con Gamberetti e Limone • *Rice with Shrimp and Lemon* 90

Risotto Primavera • *Spring Risotto* 92

Risotto con Porcini • *Risotto with Porcini Mushrooms* 94

Many years ago when I lived in London and was just learning how to feed myself like an adult, I found a little dog-eared cookbook at a secondhand bookstore. In addition to standard Italian fare such as spaghetti marinara, potatoes parmigiana and cantaloupe with prosciutto ("chill 1 small cantaloupe, cut into wedges, remove seeds and serve with prosciutto") was a recipe for rice alla Milanese. There were six ingredients and five lines of instructions. It looked, as the English taught me to say, "dead easy," and it was. I tasted it and fell in love with my first risotto. If someone had told me that risotto was tricky to make successfully, I probably wouldn't have attempted it. But they didn't, and I did – and so can you.

While entire books are now devoted to the subject, there remain only a few really important things you need to make great risotto: the best short-grained Arborio rice you can afford; an observant eye and ear to monitor heat levels and the consistency of the rice; and a little patience. You don't need special skills, culinary expertise or your own chef. You do need enough of a commitment to authenticity that you will be compelled to purchase the best ingredients.

Risotto is simply a rice dish which, while having a creamy consistency overall retains at its heart a firm (*al dente*) bite. It is rice that is coaxed towards cooking, not boiled. To achieve this, hot stock is added in stages, about half a cup (125 mL) at a time, while you stir. As you near the end of the cooking time (between 20 and 30 minutes), you will add a little less stock each time. Generally, individual flavorings – such as cheese, fresh herbs or vegetables – are added towards the very end.

With all of the above in mind, this collection of some of my favorite risotto recipes has been designed to ensure that the instructions are concise and simple.

Check the information on Arborio rice in "Necessities of the Italian Pantry" (see page 12).

Here's a rich-tasting risotto designed for lovers of Italian gorgonzola. Make sure that you trim the radicchio to remove the white stalk; otherwise the risotto may become too bitter tasting.

Risotto al Radicchio e Gorgonzola

Rice with Radicchio and Gorgonzola

6 cups	homemade or high-quality prepared beef stock (approximate)	1.5 L
1/4 cup	extra virgin olive oil	50 mL
2 tbsp	butter	25 mL
1	onion, finely chopped	1
3 cups	coarsely chopped radicchio *or* Swiss chard *or* spinach	750 mL
2 cups	short-grained Italian Arborio rice	500 mL
1/2 cup	dry white wine	125 mL
1 1/4 cups	diced Italian gorgonzola	300 mL
2 tbsp	chopped flat-leaf parsley	25 mL
1 tbsp	unsalted butter	15 mL
	Salt and freshly ground black pepper	

1. In a large saucepan, bring beef stock to a boil. Reduce heat to a slow simmer and keep the stock at this steady, slightly bubbling state throughout the rest of the cooking.

2. In a heavy-bottomed saucepan, heat olive oil and 2 tbsp (25 mL) butter over medium-high heat. Add onion and cook for 2 minutes or until translucent. Stir in radicchio; cook for 2 minutes longer. Add rice all at once; cook, stirring, for 2 minutes or until grains are well-coated with butter and oil. Pour in wine; cook, stirring, for 1 minute or until wine is absorbed.

3. Using a ladle, start to add simmering stock 1/2 cup
    (125 mL) at a time. As each ladle of stock is added,
    stir the rice to keep it from sticking to bottom and
    sides of saucepan; do not add more stock until last
    addition is absorbed. If the stock is absorbed too
    quickly, reduce the heat to maintain a slow, steady
    simmer. Repeat this process, ladling in the hot stock
    and stirring, for 15 minutes. As you near the end of
    the cooking time, reduce the amount of stock to
    1/4 cup (50 mL) at a time.

4. Continue to cook, adding more stock as necessary,
    until the rice is tender but with a firm heart and
    overall creaminess; it should not be soupy or runny-
    looking. A minute before completion, stir in gor-
    gonzola, parsley and 1 tbsp (15 mL) butter. Season
    to taste with salt and pepper. Serve immediately.

Perhaps the best-loved of all risotto because of the brilliant color imparted by the saffron, this is also one of the simplest to make. Little packets of saffron are available at many supermarkets; or look for it at specialty food shops.

Risotto alla Milanese

Saffron Risotto

6 cups	homemade or high-quality prepared chicken stock (approximate)	1.5 L
1/2 tsp	saffron	2 mL
1/4 cup	extra virgin olive oil	50 mL
2 tbsp	butter	25 mL
1	onion, finely chopped	1
2 tbsp	diced pancetta (optional)	25 mL
2	cloves garlic, minced	2
2 cups	short-grained Italian Arborio rice	500 mL
1/2 cup	dry white wine	125 mL
1/2 cup	grated Parmigiano-Reggiano	125 mL
1 tbsp	unsalted butter	15 mL
	Salt and freshly ground black pepper	

1. In a large saucepan, bring chicken stock to a boil. Reduce heat to a slow simmer and keep the stock at this steady, slightly bubbling state throughout the rest of the cooking. Use 1/2 cup (125 mL) of the hot stock to dissolve saffron; set aside.

2. In a heavy-bottomed saucepan, heat olive oil and 2 tbsp (25 mL) butter over medium-high heat. Add onion and, if using, pancetta; cook for 2 minutes or until onion is translucent. Stir in garlic; cook for 2 minutes longer. Add rice all at once; cook, stirring, for 2 minutes or until grains are well-coated with butter and oil. Pour in wine; cook, stirring, for 1 minute or until wine is absorbed.

3. Using a ladle, start to add simmering stock 1/2 cup (125 mL) at a time. As each ladle of stock is added, stir the rice to keep it from sticking to bottom and sides of saucepan; do not add more stock until last addition is absorbed. If the stock is absorbed too quickly, reduce the heat to maintain a slow, steady simmer. Repeat this process, ladling in the hot stock and stirring, for 15 minutes. As you near the end of the cooking time, reduce the amount of stock to 1/4 cup (50 mL) at a time. Stir in saffron-stock mixture.

4. Continue to cook, adding more stock as necessary, until the rice is tender but with a firm heart and overall creaminess. It should not be soupy or runny-looking. A minute before completion, stir in Parmigiano-Reggiano and 1 tbsp (15 mL) butter. Season to taste with salt and pepper. Serve immediately.

SERVES 4 TO 6

Chef Massimo Capra, of Toronto's Mistura, developed this contemporary vegetable risotto — brilliant in color and taste. You may use chicken stock if you wish, but the vegetable stock produces a lighter, less dense risotto.

Risotto Rosso di Barbabietola

Red Beet Risotto

6 cups	homemade or high-quality prepared vegetable stock (approximate)	1.5 L
1/4 cup	extra virgin olive oil	50 mL
1	onion, finely chopped	1
4	cloves garlic, oven-roasted *or* fresh, finely chopped	4
2 cups	short-grained Italian Arborio rice	500 mL
1 cup	dry white wine	250 mL
4	medium raw beets, peeled and grated, juice reserved	4
2 cups	coarsely chopped Swiss chard greens	500 mL
1 tbsp	butter	15 mL
	Grated Parmigiano-Reggiano	
	Salt and freshly ground black pepper	

1. In a large saucepan, bring vegetable stock to a boil. Reduce heat to a slow simmer and keep the stock at this steady, slightly bubbling state throughout the rest of the cooking.

2. In a heavy-bottomed saucepan, heat olive oil over medium-high heat. Add onion and cook for 2 minutes or until translucent. If using fresh garlic, add to saucepan and cook for 2 minutes longer. (Roasted garlic is added in step 4.) Add rice all at once; cook, stirring, for 2 minutes or until grains are well-coated with butter and oil. Pour in wine; cook, stirring, for 2 minutes or until wine is absorbed. Stir in beets.

3. Using a ladle, start to add simmering stock 1/2 cup (125 mL) at a time. As each ladle of stock is added, stir the rice to keep it from sticking to bottom and sides of saucepan; do not add more until last addition is absorbed. If the stock is absorbed too quickly, reduce the heat to maintain a slow, steady simmer. Repeat this process, ladling in the hot stock and stirring, for 15 minutes. As you near the end of the cooking time, reduce the amount of stock to 1/4 cup (50 mL) at a time.

4. Stir in Swiss chard and, if using, roasted garlic. Continue to cook, adding more stock as necessary, until the rice is tender but with a firm heart and overall creaminess. It should not be soupy or runny-looking. A minute before completion, stir in butter and Parmigiano-Reggiano to taste. Season to taste with salt and pepper. Serve immediately.

SERVES 4 TO 6

While risotto is originally a Northern Italian specialty (most Arborio rice is grown in Piedmont's Po Valley), I tasted this dish in a small restaurant in Lecce, in southern Italy. I can still taste the small, firm, flavorful shrimp accentuated with intense Meyer lemon.

Risotto con Gamberetti e Limone

Rice with Shrimp and Lemon

6 cups	homemade or high-quality prepared chicken stock (approximate)	1.5 L
1/4 cup	extra virgin olive oil	50 mL
2 tbsp	butter	25 mL
1	onion, finely chopped	1
2	cloves garlic, minced	2
2 cups	short-grained Italian Arborio rice	500 mL
1/2 cup	dry white wine	125 mL
12 oz	small uncooked shrimp, peeled	375 g
1	large lemon, finely grated and juiced	1
2 tbsp	chopped flat-leaf parsley	25 mL
1 tbsp	butter	15 mL
	Salt and freshly ground black pepper	

1. In a large saucepan, bring chicken stock to a boil. Reduce heat to a slow simmer and keep the stock at this steady, slightly bubbling state throughout the rest of the cooking.

2. In a heavy-bottomed saucepan, heat olive oil and 2 tbsp (25 mL) butter over medium-high heat. Add onion and cook for 2 minutes or until translucent. Stir in garlic; cook for 2 minutes longer. Add rice all at once; cook, stirring, for 2 minutes or until grains are well coated with butter and oil. Pour in wine; cook, stirring for 1 minute or until wine is absorbed. Stir in shrimp and grated lemon zest; cook, stirring, for 3 minutes.

3. Using a ladle, start to add simmering stock 1/2 cup (125 mL) at a time. As each ladle of stock is added, stir the rice to keep it from sticking to bottom and sides of saucepan; do not add more until last addition is absorbed. If the stock is absorbed too quickly, reduce the heat to maintain a slow, steady simmer. Repeat this process, ladling in the hot stock and stirring, for 15 minutes. As you near the end of the cooking time, reduce the amount of stock to 1/4 cup (50 mL) at a time.

4. Continue to cook, adding more stock as necessary, until the rice is tender but with a firm heart and overall creaminess. It should not be soupy or runny-looking. A minute before completion, stir in lemon juice, parsley and butter. Season to taste with salt and pepper. Serve immediately.

The vegetables used here can be varied according to availability but should always include tiny new peas.

Risotto Primavera

Spring Risotto

6	asparagus spears, trimmed, cut into 1-inch (2.5 cm) lengths	6
1 cup	peas (fresh or frozen)	250 mL
6 cups	homemade or high-quality prepared chicken stock (approximate)	1.5 L
1/4 cup	extra virgin olive oil	50 mL
2 tbsp	butter	25 mL
1	onion, finely chopped	1
2	cloves garlic, minced	2
2 cups	short-grained Italian Arborio rice	500 mL
1/2 cup	dry white wine	125 mL
1	small yellow zucchini, washed, trimmed and diced	1
1	small green zucchini, washed, trimmed and diced	1
1 cup	grated Parmigiano-Reggiano	250 mL
2 tbsp	chopped fresh basil	25 mL
2 tbsp	chopped flat-leaf parsley	25 mL
	Salt and freshly ground black pepper	

1. In a large pot of lightly salted boiling water, cook asparagus and, if using, fresh peas for 2 minutes or until tender-crisp. (Frozen peas are added in step 5.) Drain and refresh under cold running water; drain and set aside.

2. In a large saucepan, bring chicken stock to a boil. Reduce heat to a slow simmer and keep the stock at this steady, slightly bubbling state throughout the rest of the cooking.

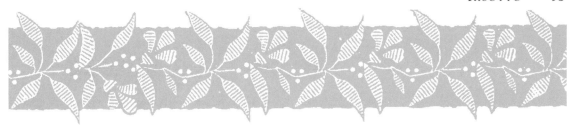

3. In a heavy-bottomed saucepan, heat olive oil and butter over medium-high heat. Add onion and cook for 2 minutes or until translucent. Stir in garlic; cook for 2 minutes longer. Add rice all at once; cook, stirring, for 2 minutes or until grains are well coated with butter and oil. Pour in wine; cook, stirring, for 1 minute or until wine is absorbed.

4. Using a ladle, start to add simmering stock 1/2 cup (125 mL) at a time. As each ladle of stock is added, stir the rice to keep it from sticking to bottom and sides of saucepan; do not add more until last addition is absorbed. If the stock is absorbed too quickly, reduce the heat to maintain a slow, steady simmer. Repeat this process, ladling in the hot stock and stirring, for 15 minutes. As you near the end of the cooking time, reduce the amount of stock to 1/4 cup (50 mL) at a time.

5. Stir in asparagus, zucchini and, if using, frozen peas. Continue to cook, adding more stock as necessary, until the rice is tender but with a firm heart and overall creaminess. It should not be soupy or runny-looking. A minute before completion, stir in Parmigiano-Reggiano, basil and parsley. Season to taste with salt and pepper. Serve immediately.

SERVES 6

Add red wine just before the stock to make this hearty risotto. You'll need good-quality dried porcini to make it great.

Risotto con Porcini

Risotto with Porcini Mushrooms

2 oz	dried porcini mushrooms	50 g
6 cups	homemade or high-quality prepared chicken stock (approximate)	1.5 L
1/4 cup	extra virgin olive oil	50 mL
2 tbsp	butter	25 mL
1	red onion, finely chopped	1
2	cloves garlic, minced	2
2 cups	short-grained Italian Arborio rice	500 mL
1/2 cup	dry red wine	125 mL
1/2 cup	grated Parmigiano-Reggiano	125 mL
3 tbsp	finely chopped flat-leaf parsley	45 mL
1 tbsp	butter	15 mL
	Salt and freshly ground black pepper	

1. In a bowl combine porcini mushrooms with warm water to cover; let stand 30 minutes. Drain. Rinse mushrooms and chop roughly. Set aside.

2. In a large saucepan, bring chicken stock to a boil. Reduce heat to a slow simmer and keep the stock at this steady, slightly bubbling state throughout the rest of the cooking.

3. In a heavy-bottomed saucepan, heat olive oil and butter over medium-high heat. Add onion and cook for 2 minutes or until translucent. Stir in garlic; cook for 2 minutes longer. Add rice all at once; cook, stirring, for 2 minutes or until grains are well-coated with butter and oil. Pour in wine; cook, stirring, for 1 minute or until wine is absorbed.

4. Using a ladle, start to add simmering stock 1/2 cup (125 mL) at a time. As each ladle of stock is added, stir the rice to keep it from sticking to bottom and sides of saucepan; do not add more stock until last addition is absorbed. After the first ladle of stock has been absorbed, stir in mushrooms along with second ladle of stock. Repeat this process, ladling in the hot stock and stirring, for 15 minutes. If the stock is absorbed too quickly, reduce the heat to maintain a slow, steady simmer. As you near the end of the cooking time, reduce the amount of stock to 1/4 cup (50 mL) at a time.

5. Continue to cook, adding more stock as necessary, until the rice is tender but with a firm heart and overall creaminess. It should not be soupy or runny-looking. A minute before completion, stir in Parmigiano-Reggiano, parsley and 1 tbsp (15 mL) butter. Season to taste with salt and pepper. Serve immediately.

CARNE
MEAT

BEEF

Manzo Stufato al Barolo • *Beef Pot Roast in Barolo* 98

Coda alla Vaccinara • *Oxtail Stew* 100

La Carbonnade • *Rich Beef Stew* 102

Polpettine alla Salvia • *Crisp Meat Patties with Sage* 103

VEAL

Spezzatino di Vitello • *Veal Stew with Peppers* 104

Saltimbocca • *Veal Scallops with Sage* 105

Involtini con Fagioloni Bianchi • *Stuffed Veal Rolls with White Beans* 106

Osso Buco • *Veal Shanks with Red Wine Sauce* 108

Fegato di Vitello al Balsamico • *Calves Liver with Balsamic Vinegar* 109

SALSICCIA ALL'UVA • *SAUSAGES WITH GRAPES* (PAGE 115) ➤

OVERLEAF: POLLO ALLA UMBRIA • *UMBRIAN-STYLE CHICKEN* (PAGE 138)

CARNE
MEAT

PORK

Spezzatino di Maiale • *Pork Stew* 110

Arista di Maiale con Patate • *Roast Pork with Potatoes* 111

Braciole di Maiale alla Napoletana • *Stuffed Pork Rolls* 112

Peperoni Ripieni con Salsiccia • *Peppers Stuffed with Sausage* 114

Salsiccia all'Uva • *Sausages with Grapes* 115

LAMB

Stinco d'Agnello con Purée di Fave • *Lamb Shanks with Fava Bean Purée* 116

Agnello e Peperoni • *Lamb with Peppers* 118

Agnello in Pignatta • *Lamb Stew* 120

GAME

Quaglie Arrosto con Pancetta • *Quail Roasted with Pancetta* 121

Coniglio ai Pomodoro Secchi e Salvia • *Rabbit with Sun-Dried Tomatoes and Sage* 122

◄ POLLO ALLE OLIVE • *CHICKEN WITH OLIVES* (PAGE 133)

SERVES 4

This could be the richest tasting pot roast you've ever had — just make sure to cook the beef in the same good quality Barolo that accompanies it at the table.

Manzo Stufato al Barolo

Beef Pot Roast in Barolo

2 1/2 lbs	beef (blade roast *or* other cut suitable for a pot roast)	1.25 kg
1	large onion, roughly chopped (about 1 cup [250 mL])	1
1	large carrot, roughly chopped (about 1 cup [250 mL])	1
1	stalk celery, roughly chopped (about 3/4 cup [175 mL])	1
2	large bay leaves	2
1 tsp	salt	5 mL
1/2 tsp	freshly ground black pepper	2 mL
1	bottle (750 mL) good Barolo wine	1
3 tbsp	olive oil	45 mL

1. Place the beef in a large, deep bowl. Scatter around it the onion, carrot, celery, bay leaves, salt and pepper. Pour the bottle of Barolo over the meat, turn it around a few times, cover the bowl with plastic wrap and leave to marinate in the refrigerator overnight.

2. Transfer marinated meat with tongs to a large plate and strain the wine marinade through a sieve, reserving the vegetables and bay leaves. Pour marinade into a saucepan and place over medium heat.

3. Meanwhile, in a large Dutch oven or flameproof casserole, heat olive oil over medium-high heat. Add beef and brown on all sides, turning it with tongs frequently.

4. Pour the heated wine marinade over the beef; add reserved vegetables and bay leaves. Bring to a gentle boil and cook for about 5 minutes. Reduce heat to low, cover and simmer for about 2 hours.

5. When meat is cooked, transfer to a plate with tongs. Remove beef to a cutting board. With a sharp knife, carve into 1/2-inch (1 cm) slices. Lay slices, overlapping, on a serving platter; tent with foil.

6. Purée the vegetables with a hand blender or in a food processor (or press through a sieve). Return the puréed vegetables to the liquid; stir to mix well. Boil the sauce for 10 minutes, uncovered, until thick. Pour sauce over the beef and serve immediately.

Coda alla Vaccinara

Oxtail Stew

SERVES 6

Vaccinara in Roman dialect, means "butcher style" — a description that refers to the origin of this dish. Like a number of related recipes usually made from discarded scraps, this dish was invented by slaughterhouse workers.

Oxtails take some time to cook, but the result here is a homey, satisfying meal that has few rivals for comfort food. Plan to make this dish a day in advance of serving.

3 1/2 lbs	oxtail, cut into 2-inch (5 cm) pieces, trimmed of as much fat as possible	1.75 kg
1/4 to 1/2 cup	all-purpose flour	50 to 125 mL
1/3 cup	olive oil	75 mL
1	large onion, finely chopped	1
3	carrots, scraped and finely chopped	3
3	cloves garlic, finely chopped	3
6	stalks celery, finely chopped	6
1	dried chili pepper (optional)	1
1 cup	dry red Italian wine	250 mL
1 lb	plum tomatoes (canned or fresh), peeled and roughly chopped	500 g
1/2 tsp	salt	2 mL
1/4 tsp	freshly ground black pepper	1 mL

1. In a large bowl, cover oxtail pieces with cold water and leave to soak for a few hours. Drain and rinse under cold running water, then dry thoroughly with paper towels. Dust with flour, shaking off the excess.

2. In a heavy casserole or Dutch oven, heat olive oil over medium-high heat. Add onion, carrots, garlic, half of the celery and, if using, the chili pepper; sauté until vegetables are softened, about 6 minutes.

3. Add pieces of oxtail and brown on all sides, turning frequently with tongs. Pour in the wine, increase the heat slightly, and cook at a gentle boil for about 3 minutes. Add tomatoes, stir to combine everything well and return to the boil. Reduce heat, cover and let simmer for about 5 hours, checking occasionally to make sure the sauce is not drying out. Add more wine or water if it appears to be dry.

4. When oxtails are tender, transfer with a slotted spoon to a plate. With a sieve, strain sauce into a bowl; discard solids. If sauce appears fatty, degrease somewhat. (If you have time, refrigerate the sauce and oxtails, covered, in separate bowls, overnight; the next day the fat will be easy to remove from the surface of the sauce.)

5. Return sauce and oxtails to the heat. Add remaining celery, stir and simmer for another 30 minutes or until celery is cooked. Season to taste with salt and pepper. Serve immediately.

SERVES 4 TO 6

Here's a very old, very traditional dish named after the Piedmont charcoal burners who invented it. Although this recipe originates from the Valle d'Aosta — a region of Italy where potatoes are daily fare — it is also wonderful with hot, creamy polenta.

Technically, this recipe provides enough for 6 servings, but if you are entertaining, it won't hurt to make a little extra.

This stew may be made a day ahead and reheated before serving.

La Carbonnade

Rich Beef Stew

2 1/2 lbs	good stewing beef, trimmed and cut into 1/2-inch (1 cm) strips	1.25 kg
1/4 cup	all-purpose flour	50 mL
3 tbsp	olive oil	45 mL
1	large onion, roughly chopped	1
1	bottle (750 mL) robust red Italian wine	1
1 tsp	salt	5 mL
1/2 tsp	freshly ground black pepper	2 mL

1. Dust beef strips with flour, shaking off the excess. In a Dutch oven or heavy-bottomed saucepan, heat olive oil over medium-high heat. Add beef and, in batches if necessary, brown the beef on all sides, turning frequently. Remove beef with a slotted spoon to a plate.

2. Add onion to pan (with a little more oil if necessary); cook until softened, about 5 minutes.

3. Return beef strips to pan and splash in one-quarter of the wine. Scrape up any bits from the bottom and sides of the Dutch oven; bring to a boil, reduce heat and allow to simmer.

4. As the sauce is reduced, add more wine; continue to simmer for almost 2 hours, adding all of the wine in stages and simmering the meat until it is completely tender and the sauce is thick and rich. Season to taste with salt and pepper. Serve immediately.

Polpettine alla Salvia

Crisp Meat Patties with Sage

2 lbs	lean ground beef	1 kg
1	onion, peeled and grated (about 1/2 cup [125 mL])	1
10 to 12	sage leaves, washed, patted dry and finely chopped	10 to 12
1 tsp	salt	5 mL
1/2 tsp	freshly ground black pepper	2 mL
1/4 cup	grated Parmigiano-Reggiano	50 mL
1	egg, beaten	1
1/2 cup	dry bread crumbs	125 mL
2 tbsp	butter	25 mL
2 tbsp	olive oil	25 mL
	Fresh sage leaves to garnish	

1. In a bowl combine beef, onion, sage, salt, pepper, Parmigiano-Reggiano, egg and half of the bread crumbs. Mix together gently with your hands to fully incorporate all the ingredients together. Do not overmix.

2. Shape mixture into small patties, about 1 1/2 inches (4 cm) across. Dip each patty into remaining bread crumbs. In a skillet, melt the butter over medium-high heat. Add olive oil and, when sizzling, fry patties for about 6 to 7 minutes per side. Do not crowd the skillet; work in batches if necessary.

3. Drain on paper towels and serve hot or warm, garnished with fresh sage leaves.

SERVES 6

Even though they seem to dissolve into the stew during the lengthy cooking time, it is the slow-cooked peppers that give this dish its unique flavor. It is especially nice served with FAGIOLI ALLA TOSCANA (see recipe, page 155). Vary the recipe by substituting lean stewing pork for the veal.

This may be made a day ahead and reheated before serving.

Spezzatino di Vitello

Veal Stew with Peppers

1/4 cup	olive oil	50 mL
3	cloves garlic, minced	3
2	medium onions, chopped	2
2	bay leaves	2
2 lbs	boneless veal shoulder, cut into 1 1/2-inch (4 cm) cubes	1 kg
1 cup	dry red wine	250 mL
3 cups	beef stock	750 mL
2 lbs	ripe plum tomatoes, peeled and chopped *or* canned Italian plum tomatoes, drained and chopped	1 kg
4 or 5	long yellow banana *or* cubanelle peppers, seeded and roughly chopped	4 or 5
3 tbsp	chopped flat-leaf parsley	45 mL
1/2 tsp	salt	2 mL
1/4 tsp	freshly ground black pepper	1 mL

1. In a Dutch oven or heavy casserole, heat olive oil over medium heat. Add garlic, onions and bay leaves; cook about 6 minutes or until vegetables are softened. Brown the veal in batches, stirring and turning to sear all sides.

2. Pour in the red wine, increase heat to a gentle boil and cook for about 3 minutes

3. Add beef stock, tomatoes and peppers; season with salt and pepper and stir to combine well.

4. Bring back to the boil; reduce heat, cover loosely and simmer for about 2 hours (or longer if time permits) until meat is very tender and sauce has thickened. Stir in the chopped parsley and serve.

SERVES 6

Purely Roman in origin, the word saltimbocca means "to jump in the mouth" — presumably because this dish of thin veal scallops, prosciutto and fresh sage is so irresistible that you will pop a piece into your mouth without hesitation.

Sometimes a very thin slice of mozzarella cheese is melted on top of the veal scallops just before they are served.

If you wish, substitute pork tenderloin, sliced and pounded thin, for the veal.

Saltimbocca

Veal Scallops with Sage

2 lbs	veal scallops	1 kg
4 oz	prosciutto, thinly sliced	125 g
20 to 24	sage leaves, washed and dried	20 to 24
3 tbsp	unsalted butter	45 mL
1/2 tsp	salt	2 mL
1/4 tsp	freshly ground black pepper	1 mL
3/4 cup	Marsala *or* dry white wine	175 mL

1. With a kitchen mallet or rolling pin, gently pound the veal until thin, being careful not to tear the meat. Trim each scallop to a fairly squarish shape. Lay one piece of prosciutto on top of each piece of veal, folding in the sides if necessary to make it neat.

2. Place a sage leaf at the center of each piece of prosciutto and, using a wooden cocktail stick, securely fasten the sage leaf and the prosciutto to the veal.

3. In a large skillet, melt butter over medium-high heat until sizzling. Add the veal and sauté for about 2 minutes on each side, seasoning with salt and pepper as they cook. Transfer veal to a serving platter and keep warm. Discard toothpicks.

4. Splash the Marsala into the skillet and scrape up any bits on the bottom. Bring to a gentle boil, reduce heat and simmer for a couple of minutes until sauce is glossy and slightly thickened. Pour over the veal and serve immediately.

SERVES 6

Make sure the veal you use here is as thin as possible. To achieve this, place veal slices between sheets of waxed paper and gently pound with a kitchen mallet or rolling pin, being careful not to tear the meat.

Involtini con Fagioloni Bianchi

Stuffed Veal Rolls with White Beans

Sauce

1/4 cup	olive oil	50 mL
2 oz	pancetta, chopped	50 g
3	cloves garlic, finely chopped	3
1	medium onion, finely chopped	1
1/4 cup	finely chopped flat-leaf parsley	50 mL
4	large plum tomatoes, peeled and chopped *or* canned Italian plum tomatoes, drained	4
3 cups	cooked white beans	750 mL

Filling

8 oz	mushrooms, minced	250 g
1/3 cup	dry red wine	75 mL
1/4 lb	Italian salami, finely chopped	125 g
1/3 cup	grated Parmigiano-Reggiano	75 mL
1	egg	1
1/2 tsp	salt	2 mL
1/4 tsp	freshly ground black pepper	1 mL
	Dry bread crumbs as needed	
1/4 cup	butter	50 mL
2 lbs	veal (about 12 slices)	1 kg

1. In a skillet, heat half of the olive oil over medium heat. Add pancetta, 2 of the chopped garlic cloves, the onion and half of the parsley; cook until onion is softened. Add tomatoes and beans; cook until slightly thickened, about 15 minutes. Season with salt and pepper to taste. Transfer beans/sauce mixture to a bowl; set aside.

2. Wipe the skillet clean and sauté remaining garlic in remaining olive oil. Add mushrooms and cook, stirring, for 1 minute. Add wine and cook until it is absorbed by mushrooms. Allow mushroom mixture to cool, then mix with the salami, Parmigiano-Reggiano, egg, salt and pepper. (Add a small amount of dry bread crumbs if too wet.)

3. Spread some of this mixture on each of the veal scallops. Roll slices up firmly and secure each with a toothpick. Wipe skillet clean.

4. Over medium heat, heat butter in the skillet and cook the veal rolls until golden brown, turning once or twice until cooked through, about 8 to 10 minutes. (Do not overcook, or they will toughen.) Add beans and their sauce and simmer gently until heated through, about 15 minutes. Serve immediately.

Osso Buco

Veal Shanks with Red Wine Sauce

SERVES 6

This version of the classic osso buco *is hearty, rich and red – a delicious result of the wine in which it is cooked. Serve with soft polenta or, for thorough authenticity, precede it with* RISOTTO MILANESE *(see recipe, page 86).*

1/4 cup	olive oil	50 mL
2	onions, chopped	2
6	thick veal knuckles (*osso buco*), about 10 oz (300 g) each	6
1/4 cup	all-purpose flour	50 mL
1 1/4 cups	dry red wine	300 mL
1 cup	black olives, pitted	250 mL
1 1/2 cups	*passata* (puréed, sieved tomatoes) *or* ground tomatoes	375 mL
1 cup	beef stock	250 mL
1/2 tsp	salt	2 mL
1/4 tsp	freshly ground black pepper	1 mL
1 tbsp	grated lemon zest	15 mL
1/3 cup	chopped flat-leaf parsley	75 mL

1. In a Dutch oven or heavy casserole, heat olive oil over medium-high heat. Add onions; cook until softened, about 5 minutes. Dust veal with flour, shaking off the excess. Brown veal on all sides, turning frequently with tongs, for about 10 minutes. Transfer to a plate.

2. Add red wine to casserole; increase heat and start scraping up any bits from the bottom and sides. Gently boil for about 3 minutes.

3. Stir in olives, tomatoes and beef stock. Add browned veal and, turning it over once or twice, bring to a gentle boil; reduce heat, cover and let cook gently for 1 1/2 hours, or until veal is tender and sauce is nicely thickened. Season to taste with salt and pepper. Serve sprinkled with lemon zest and chopped parsley.

SERVES 6

Nothing but calves (veal) liver should be used for this simple, almost delicate dish, which hails from beautiful Emilia-Romagna, where balsamic vinegar is produced. Serve with crispy oven-roasted potatoes and whole green beans.

Use the best quality balsamic vinegar to give the sauce a subtle sweet-sour taste.

Fegato di Vitello al Balsamico

Calves Liver with Balsamic Vinegar

1 1/2 lbs	calves liver, very thinly sliced	750 g
1/4 cup	all-purpose flour	50 mL
1/4 cup	butter	50 mL
1/2 tsp	salt	2 mL
1/4 tsp	freshly ground black pepper	1 mL
1/3 cup	balsamic vinegar	75 mL
3 tbsp	finely chopped sage	45 mL

1. Lightly dust liver in flour, shaking off the excess. In a skillet large enough to hold all the pieces, melt butter over heat until sizzling. Add liver and sauté for 1 1/2 minutes on each side or until cooked, but still pink inside. Season with salt and pepper. Transfer liver to warm platter.

2. Add vinegar to pan and scrape up any brown bits. Bring to a boil and cook 1 or 2 minutes until thickened. Return liver to pan. Turn it over once or twice and cook for another 1 or 2 minutes. Add sage and serve liver with sauce poured over.

Originally made with wild boar, this stew makes an ideal supper for those dark days of mid-winter. Polenta makes a natural accompaniment, although potatoes mashed with a little olive oil are equally good.

Spezzatino di Maiale

Pork Stew

3 tbsp	olive oil	45 mL
3 lbs	lean stewing pork, cut into 2-inch (5 cm) chunks	1.5 kg
3	cloves garlic, minced	3
1	onion, finely chopped	1
1	celery stalk, finely chopped	1
2	carrots, scraped and finely chopped	2
1/4 cup	chopped flat-leaf parsley	50 mL
3 tbsp	chopped pancetta	45 mL
2	branches fresh rosemary, leaves only, finely chopped	2
1 cup	robust dry red wine	250 mL
1/2 cup	beef stock	125 mL
1 1/2 cups	canned Italian plum tomatoes, chopped, with juice	375 mL
1/2 tsp	red pepper flakes (optional)	2 mL
1/2 tsp	salt	2 mL
1/4 tsp	freshly ground black pepper	1 mL

1. In a Dutch oven or large skillet, heat olive oil over medium heat. Add pork and, in batches if necessary, brown on all sides, transferring to a plate or bowl when done.

2. Add garlic, onion, celery, carrots, parsley, pancetta, rosemary and, if necessary, another 1 tbsp (15 mL) of olive oil; sauté for about 5 minutes.

3. Return pork to the pan and mix to combine well with the vegetables and herbs. Add red wine; cook for about 5 minutes. Add stock and cook for another 5 minutes.

4. Add tomatoes and their juice, red pepper flakes, salt and pepper; stir and bring to a gentle boil. Immediately reduce heat and simmer stew until sauce is thickened and meat is tender, about 1 1/2 hours.

Because today's pork is so lean, you can easily dry it out while cooking. But this northern Italian method will ensure that the meat stays juicy and moist. If you find the combination of cloves and rosemary too intense, omit the cloves.

Arista di Maiale con Patate

Roast Pork with Potatoes

PREHEAT OVEN TO 425° C (220° F)
ROASTING PAN WITH RACK

2 tbsp	whole black peppercorns	25 mL
6	branches rosemary, leaves only, finely chopped	6
1 tbsp	coarse salt	15 mL
3 lbs	boneless loin of pork	1.5 kg
1 tbsp	whole cloves (optional)	15 mL
2 1/2 to 3 lbs	potatoes, peeled and cut into large chunks	1.25 to 1.5 kg
6	cloves garlic, smashed	6
1 tbsp	olive oil	15 mL
1/2 tsp	salt	2 mL
1/4 tsp	freshly ground black pepper	1 mL
1 1/2 cups	dry white wine	375 mL

1. With a mortar and pestle, crack peppercorns. (Or wrap peppercorns in a tea towel and smash with kitchen mallet or rolling pin until cracked.) Mix cracked peppercorns together with chopped rosemary and salt; press mixture all over the surface of the roast. Insert cloves, if using, randomly into the roast. Toss potatoes with garlic, olive oil, salt and pepper. Place in roasting pan around the rack. Roast for about 30 minutes.

2. Reduce heat to 375° F (190° C). Place roast on rack in roasting pan with potatoes. Roast together for about 50 minutes. Add white wine and cook for another 50 minutes.

3. Remove roast from oven and allow meat to sit for 10 minutes before carving. Serve with potatoes and roasting pan juices.

SERVES 6

These savory pork rolls are stuffed with a mixture that's a favorite in Italy – raisins, pine nuts and capers. At one time in Sicily, almond paste would also have been added.

Whichever cut of pork you use, make sure to pound it so that the pieces are uniformly thin, flat and squarish. This will make them much easier to fill and roll.

Braciole di Maiale alla Napoletana

Stuffed Pork Rolls

2 lbs	boneless pork loin, sliced into 8 pieces *or* 8 boneless pork cutlets	1 kg

Stuffing

4	cloves garlic, finely chopped	4
1/4 cup	golden raisins, soaked in hot water, drained and patted dry	50 mL
1/4 cup	pine nuts	50 mL
3 tbsp	capers	45 mL
	Finely grated zest of 1 large orange	
3 tbsp	extra virgin olive oil	45 mL
2 tbsp	fresh bread crumbs	25 mL
1/2 tsp	salt	2 mL
1/4 tsp	freshly ground black pepper	1 mL
1/2 cup	chicken stock	125 mL
1/2 cup	*passata* (puréed, sieved tomatoes) *or* ground plum tomatoes	125 mL
2 tbsp	chopped fresh oregano	25 mL

1. Place the pieces of pork between sheets of waxed paper and gently pound with a kitchen mallet until thin and flat (about 1/4 inch [5 mm] thick).

2. Using a sharp knife or in a food processor, chop together the garlic, raisins, pine nuts, capers and orange zest. Add 1 tbsp (15 mL) of the extra virgin olive oil and bread crumbs. Mix together to form a paste-like mixture.

3. Lay the pieces of meat on a work surface; lightly season with salt and pepper. Place a generous tablespoon (15 mL) of the raisin and pine nut mixture on each piece of meat, centering it so that you will still be able to fold in the edges of the meat when you roll it up. Roll each one up and tie with kitchen string.

4. In a large skillet, heat remaining olive oil. Add pork rolls and brown on all sides. In a small bowl, combine the chicken stock with the *passata*, mix well and pour over pork rolls. Add a little more salt and pepper to taste, cover and cook over low heat, turning once or twice, for 1 to 1 1/2 hours.

5. Transfer pork roll to a warmed platter and carefully remove kitchen string. Pour sauce over the rolls; sprinkle with fresh oregano and serve.

Serve this effortless dish either as antipasto or a light first course. Use the best quality, lean Italian sausage – sweet or spicy. Serve with good crusty bread.

This dish looks pretty if you use a mixture of red, green or yellow peppers.

Peperoni Ripieni con Salsiccia

Peppers Stuffed with Sausage

PREHEAT OVEN TO 400° F (200° C)
BAKING SHEET

1 1/2 cups	fresh bread crumbs	375 mL
1/2 cup	milk	125 mL
3	bell peppers, any color	3
1 tbsp	olive oil	15 mL
1 lb	Italian sausage, slit open and skins removed	500 g
1	egg	1
1/2 tsp	salt	2 mL
1/4 tsp	freshly ground black pepper	1 mL
3 tbsp	chopped flat-leaf parsley	45 mL
	Extra virgin olive oil	

1. In a bowl soak bread crumbs in milk. Halve peppers lengthwise, trim and seed, leaving the stems intact. Brush baking sheet with olive oil and bake peppers on it for about 10 to 15 minutes. Remove from oven and allow to cool. (Leave oven on.)

2. Using your hands, squeeze bread crumbs and allow excess milk to drain into bowl.

3. In another bowl, combine softened bread crumbs with sausage, egg, salt, pepper and parsley. Mix gently with fork until combined. Do not overmix.

4. Stuff peppers with mixture and bake for about 20 minutes. Serve drizzled with extra virgin olive oil.

Here's a dish that will be the star of a late-summer al fresco supper. Use your barbecue or grill to cook the sausages.

Salsiccia all'Uva

Sausages with Grapes

PREHEAT GRILL OR START BARBECUE

2 lbs	hot Italian sausage (lean, high quality)	1 kg
1 lb	seedless green grapes	500 g
1 lb	seedless red grapes	500 g
2 tbsp	olive oil	25 mL

1. Grill sausages over medium-high heat until cooked through. In a skillet, heat olive oil. Add grapes and toss over medium heat until plumped and heated through, about 2 minutes. (Alternatively, pan-fry sausages in a little olive oil; remove after 15 minutes or when cooked, add grapes to pan and follow instructions above.)

SERVES 6

Chef Massimo Capra of Mistura tells me that in Apulia, the fava bean purée and chicory included here would be served first on their own, followed by the lamb and its sauce teamed with boiled potatoes. However you choose to serve it, this is one outstanding preparation.

Plan to make the bean purée the day before.

To save time and effort, buy skinned, dried fava beans. Simply rinse, cover with cold water and bring to a boil; turn heat off and let stand 1 hour. Purée and proceed with recipe as described in step 3.

Stinco d'Agnello con Purée di Fave

Lamb Shanks with Fava Bean Purée

3 tbsp	olive oil	45 mL
6	lamb shanks	6
2	carrots, scraped and chopped	2
2	onions, chopped	2
3	stalks celery, chopped	3
4	bay leaves	4
5	branches rosemary	5
1 1/2 cups	dry white wine	375 mL
2 tbsp	butter	25 mL
	Salt and freshly ground black pepper to taste	
6 cups	chicken stock	1.5 L

Fava bean purée

1 lb	whole dried fava beans, soaked overnight and drained	500 g
3	garlic cloves, finely chopped	3
1/2 tsp	salt	2 mL
1/4 cup	olive oil	50 mL
1 lb	broccoli rabe (*or* other bitter greens such as dandelion, turnip or collard greens), chopped and blanched	500 g
3 tbsp	extra virgin olive oil	45 mL

1. In a casserole or Dutch oven, heat olive oil over high heat. Add lamb shanks and sear until golden brown. Add carrots, onions, celery, bay leaves, rosemary, salt and pepper; continue cooking for a few minutes. Add wine and cook for 5 minutes to allow alcohol to evaporate. Add half of the stock and simmer, covered, for 1 1/2 hours over very low heat.

2. Meanwhile, make the fava purée: Pull outer skin off each fava bean. Place peeled beans and garlic in a saucepan, add fresh water to cover and cook until tender, about 1 hour, skimming off any foam that rises to the surface. When foam stops appearing, add salt; stir beans occasionally with a wooden spoon to help them break up. Keep some water boiling to add to the beans as they cook to keep them from sticking to the bottom of the pan.

3. Once the beans are completely cooked, mash them to a purée with the olive oil. (Alternatively, put them through a food mill or into a food processor and blend with olive oil until smooth.) Season to taste.

4. When meat is tender, carefully remove it to a warm serving platter; cover and set to one side. Keep lamb warm. Bring liquid to a boil and cook until reduced by one-third (about 1 hour). Add butter and season to taste. Strain liquid through a fine sieve into a small saucepan; keep warm.

5. In a skillet heat the remaining olive oil over medium heat. Add the chopped, blanched greens and a little salt and pepper; sauté until slightly wilted.

6. To serve, place one scoop of bean purée and greens in the center of a rimmed pasta plate. Top with one lamb shank and pour the juices around the vegetables. Serve immediately.

The green hills of Abruzzi and Molise are resplendent with wild thyme and other herbs. With such ideal grazing conditions, it's little wonder that these regions are famous for their lamb. Here the food is characterized by strong flavors, fresh herbs and il diavoletto (hot peppers) – all of which are featured in this recipe.

You can prepare the dish a day ahead with good results. Be sure to allow enough time (overnight if possible) to marinate the lamb.

If shoulder of lamb is not available, use boneless leg of lamb and reduce final cooking time by about 30 minutes.

Agnello e Peperoni

Lamb with Peppers

2 cups	dry white wine	500 mL
2 tbsp	crumbled thyme	25 mL
3 tbsp	olive oil	45 mL
3	cloves garlic, finely chopped	3
1 tbsp	grated lemon zest	15 mL
3 lbs	boneless shoulder of lamb, trimmed of excess fat, cut into 1-inch (2.5 cm) chunks	1.5 kg
1/4 cup	olive oil	50 mL
1	large onion, chopped	1
3 tbsp	chopped flat-leaf parsley	45 mL
2	dried hot chilies, crumbled (use rubber gloves when handling)	2
3	cloves garlic, finely chopped	3
1 cup	*passata* (puréed, sieved tomatoes) *or* canned ground or crushed tomatoes	250 mL
1 1/2 cups	chicken stock	375 mL
3/4 tsp	salt	4 mL
1/4 tsp	freshly ground black pepper	1 mL
2	red bell peppers, seeded and cut into strips	2
1	yellow bell pepper, seeded and cut into strips	1
1	green pepper, seeded and cut into strips	1

1. In a large bowl, whisk together the white wine, thyme, 3 tbsp (45 mL) of oil, garlic and lemon zest. Add chunks of lamb and toss to coat. Cover with plastic wrap and refrigerate 8 hours or overnight.

2. In a large heavy casserole or Dutch oven, heat olive oil over medium heat. With tongs, transfer lamb to a plate lined with a few thicknesses of paper towel. (Reserve marinade.) Pat lamb dry and brown in batches in casserole, transferring to a bowl when done. Add more oil as needed to finish browning lamb.

3. Add chopped onion, parsley, chilies and garlic; sauté for a few minutes or until onion is softened. (Do not allow garlic to brown.) Add reserved marinade and bring to a boil, scraping up any brown bits. Add cooked lamb, tomatoes, stock, salt and pepper; return to a boil. Reduce heat and simmer mixture for 1 1/2 to 2 hours or until meat is tender.

4. Just before the lamb is completely cooked, warm a little more olive oil in a nonstick skillet. Add strips of peppers and sauté for about 3 minutes or until slightly cooked but not softened. Add to casserole and allow lamb to simmer for another few minutes. Serve with plenty of crusty bread.

A pignatta is a rustic two-handled terra cotta pot or casserole dish popular throughout Italy. Because it has no lid, a cover would often be fashioned from bread dough – quite necessary when you consider that the traditional way of slow-cooking stew was to bury the vessel in hot embers. Today, of course, we can simply use a lidded casserole.

While North Americans usually think of curly greens like escarole as a salad ingredient, Italians also enjoy escarole, or ciccoria, as a cooked vegetable.

Agnello in Pignatta

Lamb Stew

PREHEAT OVEN TO 350° C (180° F)
16-CUP (4 L) CASSEROLE WITH LID

3 lbs	lamb, cut into 2-inch (5 cm) chunks	1.5 kg
6	potatoes, (suitable for boiling), peeled and quartered	6
2	onions, quartered	2
2	carrots, scraped and cut into chunks	2
1	head escarole, washed, drained and coarsely chopped	1
1/2 tsp	salt	2 mL
1/4 tsp	freshly ground black pepper	1 mL
1	sprig rosemary	1
2 cups	beef stock	500 mL
2 cups	red wine	500 mL

1. Put lamb, potatoes, onions, carrots and escarole in casserole; mix together. Sprinkle over salt and pepper. Add rosemary sprig.

2. In a mixing bowl, blend together beef stock and wine. Pour over lamb mixture. Cover with lid. Bake in preheated oven for 2 to 2 1/2 hours or until lamb is tender.

Quaglie Arrosto con Pancetta

Quail Roasted with Pancetta

PREHEAT OVEN TO 400° F (200° C)

10	quail	10
10	sprigs sage	10
10	cloves garlic, peeled and left whole	10
4 oz	butter, softened	125 g
1/2 tsp	salt	2 mL
1/4 tsp	freshly ground black pepper to taste	1 mL
10	slices pancetta (Italian bacon), unrolled	10
	Wedges of lemon	

1. Wipe clean each quail, inside and out. Pat dry with paper towel. Place a sprig of sage and a clove of garlic inside the cavity of each quail, along with a small knob of the butter.

2. Spread the remaining butter over each quail's breast and legs. Season with salt and pepper. Wrap each one with a strip of pancetta. (You may wish to secure the pancetta with a toothpick.)

3. Place birds in a roasting pan and roast in preheated oven for about 15 minutes. Remove from oven and let rest for 5 minutes. Serve with a squeeze of fresh lemon.

Rabbit is a popular meat in Italy, where it is cooked in a variety of ways. While many traditional recipes were designed for strong-tasting wild hare, today's farm-raised rabbit is mild, tender and requires much less time to cook. Ask your butcher to cut the rabbit up for you.

While commercially prepared sun-dried tomatoes are widely available, you can also make your own oven-dried tomatoes. They add a beautiful dimension of flavor and color to this recipe – and many others – and they're a snap to make. Preheat oven to 300 °F (150° C). Drizzle a little olive oil over 2 baking sheets. Halve 16 plum tomatoes lengthwise. With a spoon or sharp knife, carefully remove the pulp and seeds. Arrange the cut tomatoes on sheets, making sure they are not touching each other. Drizzle with a very little bit more olive oil and sprinkle sparingly with salt and sugar. Dry in oven for about 1 hour. Remove and leave to cool. When they are completely dry, store in airtight jar or plastic bag. They will also keep indefinitely packed in a jar and covered with extra virgin olive oil and used as needed. The resulting tomato-infused olive oil is fabulous as a vinaigrette base, tossed with fresh pasta, drizzled over grilled vegetables or used to sauté boneless breasts of chicken or fish fillets.

May be made a day ahead and re-heated.

Coniglio ai Pomodoro Secchi e Salvia

Rabbit with Sun-Dried Tomatoes and Sage

4 lbs	rabbit, cut into pieces	2 kg
1/4 cup	all-purpose flour	50 mL
2 tbsp	olive oil	25 mL
1	small carrot, scraped and chopped	1
1	stalk celery, chopped	1
1	onion, chopped	1
3	cloves garlic, finely chopped	3
1/2 tsp	salt	2 mL
1/4 tsp	freshly ground black pepper	1 mL
1 cup	dry white wine	250 mL
2 tbsp	balsamic vinegar	25 mL
1 cup	chicken stock (approximate)	250 mL
12	sage leaves	12
10	oven-dried tomato halves (see technique at left) *or* commercial sun-dried tomatoes	10
1/2 cup	black olives (pitted if desired)	125 mL

1. Dust rabbit pieces with flour, shaking off any excess. In a heavy skillet, heat oil over medium heat. Add rabbit pieces, in batches if necessary, and brown on all sides, about 20 minutes.

2. Return rabbit pieces to the pan; add carrot, celery, onion, garlic, salt, pepper, wine and balsamic vinegar. Bring to a gentle boil; cook for about 10 minutes. Add chicken stock; return to boil; reduce heat to low and cook, covered, for about 45 minutes or until rabbit is tender. (Add more chicken stock if rabbit gets too dry.)

3. Remove rabbit pieces to a heated serving platter. Keep warm. In a food processor or blender, purée the juices and cooked vegetables until smooth. Stir in sage leaves, dried tomatoes and black olives; cook 2 minutes or just until heated through. Pour sauce over meat and serve immediately.

POLLO
CHICKEN

SERVES 4 TO 6

I never much cared for conventional chicken cacciatore, probably because I wasn't a fan of the combination of chicken and tomatoes. But this version is different. The Tuscan style eases up on the tomatoes and relies more on the qualities of a good Italian red wine (don't stint!) – with outstanding results.

While I have made this recipe with white and/or dark meat, the most successful version was made with humble chicken thighs. Remove their skin but keep them on the bone to ensure the most flavor.

Pollo Cacciatore alla Toscana

Chicken Tuscan Hunter Style

1/4 cup	olive oil	50 mL
4	garlic cloves, finely chopped	4
1	branch rosemary, leaves only, finely chopped	1
12	sage leaves, finely chopped	12
4 1/2 lbs	chicken thighs, skin removed	2.25 kg
1/2 tsp	salt	2 mL
1/4 tsp	freshly ground black pepper	1 mL
1 cup	dry red wine	250 mL
2 tbsp	tomato paste	25 mL
1 1/2 cups	chicken stock	375 mL

1. In a large skillet, heat olive oil over medium heat. Add garlic, rosemary and sage; cook for 1 or 2 minutes. Add chicken, in batches if necessary, and sear on both sides; continue cooking until chicken is golden brown, about 15 minutes.

2. Season chicken with salt and pepper. Splash in the red wine. Bring to a gentle boil and cook for about 5 minutes.

3. Blend the tomato paste into the stock and pour over chicken. Cover and let simmer 30 to 35 minutes or until chicken is cooked through and sauce is thickened. Serve immediately.

Petti di Pollo alla Pizzaiola

Chicken Breasts in Pizzaiola Sauce

SERVES 4 TO 6

Pizzaiola is Naples' classic tomato sauce – so named because the ingredients for this fresh-tasting, simple sauce are the same as those used to dress pizzas. This preparation is simplicity itself. The sauce can be used with pasta and is equally good with mild-tasting white fish, shrimp or seared scallops.

Try to use fresh oregano; there is no comparison between it and the dried version.

You can omit the anchovies if you prefer. If using anchovies, you may need less salt.

1/4 cup	olive oil	50 mL
4	garlic cloves, minced	4
4	anchovy fillets, rinsed, drained, patted dry and finely chopped	4
2 tbsp	finely chopped flat-leaf parsley	25 mL
2 tsp	finely chopped oregano	10 mL
2 1/2 cups	canned, peeled plum tomatoes, chopped, plus 1/4 cup (50 mL) of their juice or, in season, 2 1/2 lbs (1.25 kg) fresh, ripe plum tomatoes, chopped or *passata* (puréed, sieved tomatoes)	625 mL
1/2 tsp	salt	2 mL
1/4 tsp	freshly ground black pepper	1 mL
3 tbsp	olive oil	45 mL
6	boneless, skinless chicken breasts, pounded flat	6

1. In a skillet heat the olive oil over medium-high heat. Add garlic and cook for 1 minute or until softened. Stir in chopped anchovies, parsley, and oregano.

2. Using the back of a fork, mash the anchovies into a paste. Cook, stirring, for another 2 or 3 minutes. Add tomatoes, salt and pepper; stir until well combined. Cook until thickened, about 15 minutes.

3. In another skillet, heat remaining olive oil. Add chicken breasts and cook for about 8 minutes on each side, until cooked through.

4. Season thickened tomato sauce to taste. Pour some of the sauce to pool in the center of each warmed plate. Place a chicken breast on top of the sauce and serve immediately.

Pollo alla Salvia

Chicken with Sage

SERVES 4 TO 6

The Italians are fond of preparing chicken in a simple braise – first browning in a little oil then cooking in liquid – and have devised many variations on this theme. Here is one of the best and easiest. Try to use chicken pieces that are all more-or-less the same size. Serve with crisp, roasted potatoes and a salad of peppery greens.

2 tbsp	butter	25 mL
1/4 cup	olive oil	50 mL
1	chicken (about 4 to 5 lbs [2 to 2.5 kg]), cut into parts *or* equivalent weight of pre-cut chicken pieces	1
1 1/2 cups	dry white wine	375 mL
24	sage leaves, chopped	24
1 tsp	salt	5 mL
1/4 tsp	freshly ground black pepper	1 mL

1. In a large skillet, melt butter over medium-high heat. Add olive oil and stir to blend. Add chicken pieces, in batches if necessary, and cook until they are golden on all sides. Drain all but 1/4 cup (50 mL) of fat.

2. Return all chicken pieces to the pan, nestling them together in a single layer. Pour wine over chicken; increase heat and bring to a gentle boil. Cook for about 5 minutes.

3. Add sage, salt and pepper. Turn chicken pieces over to cover them with the sage, shaking the pan a little to help them to nestle down. Reduce heat to low, cover loosely and let it gently bubble away until chicken is cooked through and very tender, about 45 minutes. (Turn the pieces over periodically and check to make sure the liquid is not evaporating too quickly; if it is, add a little water.) Serve immediately.

SERVES 4 TO 6

Cutting open a whole chicken and flattening it, as we do here, speeds up cooking time. This is also the method used for POLLO ALLA DIAVOLA (see recipe, page 134) and works well for oven roasting or grilling.

Be sure to use lemons of the same size – too much fresh lemon juice will overpower all the other flavors and make the sauce bitter.

Pollo ai Limoni

Chicken with Lemon

1	chicken (about 4 lbs [2 kg]), cut lengthwise down back or breastbone, allowing it to lie flat	1
2 tbsp	olive oil	25 mL
3	small lemons, halved and juiced (about 3/4 cup [175 mL] juice)	3
6	cloves garlic, smashed	6
Half	bunch flat-leaf parsley, washed, dried and roughly chopped	Half
1/3 cup	chicken stock, cooled	75 mL
1/2 tsp	salt	2 mL
1/4 tsp	freshly ground black pepper	1 mL

1. Trim chicken of any excess fat and transfer to a terra cotta or casserole dish. (It should be large enough to accommodate the chicken comfortably.) Drizzle with olive oil; pour lemon juice over. Add garlic and parsley, nestling it in and around the chicken.

2. Pour stock over the chicken; season with salt and pepper. Cover loosely with plastic wrap and marinate at room temperature for about 1 hour, turning it over periodically. (If kitchen is hot, marinate in refrigerator.)

3. Preheat oven to 400° F (200° C). Remove plastic wrap. Make sure chicken is skin side up and roast in preheated oven for about 55 to 65 minutes, until chicken is cooked through, basting occasionally with the marinade. Be careful not to overcook. Remove from oven and let stand for about 5 minutes before serving.

SERVES 4 TO 6

Here's a very popular dish from Sicily, where eggplant is the winner and undefeated champion of vegetables. Any variety of eggplant may be used for this dish: the regular elongated variety; the smaller, rounder Italian type; or, the long, slender Asian eggplant.

Pollo con Melanzane e Pomodoro

Chicken with Eggplant and Tomato

PREHEAT OVEN TO 375° F (190° C)
BAKING SHEET, LIGHTLY OILED

2 lbs	eggplant, trimmed, cut into 1-inch (2.5 cm) cubes	1 kg
2 tbsp	salt	25 mL
1/4 cup	olive oil	50 mL
4	cloves garlic, chopped	4
2	stalks celery, chopped	2
2 tbsp	chopped flat-leaf parsley	25 mL
1	chicken (about 4 to 5 lbs [2 to 2.5 kg]) cut into parts *or* equivalent weight of pre-cut chicken pieces	1
1 tbsp	red pepper flakes	15 mL
1/2 tsp	salt	2 mL
1/4 tsp	freshly ground black pepper	1 mL
1 1/2 cups	dry white wine	375 mL
2 cups	canned plum tomatoes, peeled, with juice or, in season, 2 lbs (1 kg) fresh, ripe plum tomatoes, chopped or *passata* (puréed, sieved tomatoes)	500 mL
	Flat-leaf parsley, chopped	

1. Place the eggplant in a colander set in the sink and sprinkle with salt. Leave to drain for about 1 hour. Rinse and pat dry with paper towels.

2. Put eggplant on prepared baking sheet. Roast in pre-heated oven for about 20 to 25 minutes or until soft and brown.

Recipe continues…

SOGLIOLE IN SAOR • *VENETIAN SOLE* (PAGE 142) ➤
OVERLEAF: BRODETTO • *FISH STEW* (PAGE 146)

3. Meanwhile, in a large skillet, heat olive oil over medium-high heat. Add garlic, celery and parsley; cook for a few minutes or until slightly softened. In batches, add chicken pieces, sprinkling them with red pepper flakes, salt and pepper; cook, turning often, until golden brown on all sides.

4. Add white wine and bring to a gentle boil; cook for about 5 minutes. Add tomatoes, shaking the pan a little to settle them down between the chicken pieces; return to the boil. Reduce heat to low; cover loosely and simmer for about 35 minutes, stirring occasionally, until chicken is cooked through. Add a little water if sauce becomes too dry.

5. Gently combine eggplant with chicken. Transfer everything to a warmed serving platter and serve sprinkled with plenty of chopped flat-leaf parsley.

◄ PEPERONI ALLA PIEMONTESE • *PIEDMONT PEPPERS* (PAGE 154)

SERVES 4 TO 6

These neat little bundles are filled with a fragrant herbal stuffing. They can also be wrapped in pancetta before they are rolled and sautéed.

Sliced into 1-inch (2.5 cm) thick pieces, this chicken makes a nice addition to an Italian buffet.

Vary the herbs to suit your taste. Marjoram, sage or thyme may all be used in place of oregano, but try to include fresh basil and, of course, parsley.

This dish can be made ahead up to the point where the chicken is cooked.

Save the bones for making stock.

Pollo Ripieni alla Siciliana

Sicilian-Style Stuffed Chicken

Stuffing

1/2 cup	dry bread crumbs, slightly toasted	125 mL
1/2 cup	warm chicken stock	125 mL
3 tbsp	capers, drained and chopped	45 mL
2	cloves garlic, finely chopped	2
1/4 cup	green olives, pitted and chopped	50 mL
1/4 cup	chopped flat-leaf parsley	50 mL
3 tbsp	chopped basil	45 mL
3 tbsp	chopped oregano	45 mL
3 tbsp	extra virgin olive oil	45 mL
2 tbsp	pine nuts	25 mL
3 tbsp	grated Pecorino Romano or Parmigiano-Reggiano	45 mL
1/4 tsp	freshly ground black pepper	1 mL
4 lbs	boneless skinless chicken thighs	2 kg

Sauce

1/4 cup	olive oil	50 mL
2	cloves garlic, finely chopped	2
1	onion, finely chopped	1
1	carrot, scraped and finely chopped	1
1	stalk celery, finely chopped	1
1 1/2 cups	dry white wine	375 mL
1 tbsp	tomato paste	15 mL
1/2 tsp	salt	2 mL

1. In a small bowl, combine bread crumbs and stock; set aside. Meanwhile, in a medium-size bowl, combine the garlic, olives, parsley, basil, oregano, extra virgin olive oil, pine nuts, Pecorino Romano and pepper. Drain crumbs of any excess liquid and stir into stuffing mixture to a paste-like consistency.

2. Arrange chicken thighs on a clean work surface, boned side up. Fill each cavity with a heaped tablespoon (15 mL) of stuffing mixture, being careful not to overstuff. Roll up thighs from one side to the other; secure with a toothpick or tie with string.

3. In a large skillet, heat 1/4 cup (50 mL) olive oil over medium heat. Add garlic, onion, carrot and celery; cook 6 minutes or until softened. Add stuffed chicken thighs; cook, turning occasionally, 15 minutes or until browned on all sides.

4. In a small bowl, whisk together the wine, tomato paste and salt. Pour half over the chicken. Bring to a boil and cook for a few minutes; reduce heat, cover and let simmer for about 30 to 35 minutes, turning chicken occasionally. Add more wine mixture as necessary.

5. Transfer chicken to warmed serving platter; let rest for 20 minutes. Strain pan juices and vegetables through a fine sieve. Discard any solids. Return sauce to pan; heat through over very low heat.

6. Remove toothpicks or string from chicken. With a sharp knife, cut stuffed thighs on a slight diagonal into 1-inch (2.5 cm) slices. Return to serving platter, pour sauce over and serve immediately.

SERVES 4 TO 6

Oven roasting potatoes together with meat is a common practice in southern Italy – and is often applied to pork or lamb.

There is nothing complicated or even remotely sophisticated about this dish, so make sure to purchase the freshest, best quality chicken you can find. It's simply very, very good.

Pollo Asciutto

Crisp Roasted Chicken

PREHEAT OVEN TO 425° F (220° C)

6	large potatoes, suitable for roasting, peeled and cut into chunks	6
6	cloves garlic, roughly chopped	6
3 tbsp	extra virgin olive oil	45 mL
1/2 cup	chopped flat-leaf parsley	125 mL
1 tsp	salt	5 mL
1/2 tsp	freshly ground black pepper	2 mL
1	chicken (about 4 to 5 lbs [2 to 2.5 kg]), cut into parts *or* equivalent weight of pre-cut chicken pieces	1
3 tbsp	extra virgin olive oil	45 mL

1. In a roasting pan large enough to accommodate the chicken, toss the potato chunks with 1 cup (250 mL) water, garlic, 3 tbsp (45 mL) olive oil, parsley, and half of the salt and pepper. Distribute the potatoes in a single layer in pan; roast 30 minutes in preheated oven.

2. Meanwhile, in a large bowl, combine chicken with 3 tbsp (45 mL) oil; toss to coat well. Add remaining salt and pepper.

3. Remove potatoes from oven and place chicken on top. Roast on center oven rack for about 60 to 65 minutes, turning chicken and potatoes over occasionally to ensure even cooking.

4. When chicken and potatoes are crisp and golden brown, remove from oven and serve immediately.

Pollo alle Olive

Chicken with Olives

3 tbsp	olive oil	45 mL
4	cloves garlic, peeled and smashed	4
1	chicken (about 4 1/2 lbs [2.25 kg]), cut into parts *or* equivalent weight of pre-cut chicken pieces	1
1 cup	dry white wine	250 mL
2 tbsp	balsamic vinegar	25 mL
1 cup	whole black olives, pitted	250 mL
1 cup	finely chopped black olives	250 mL
1/2 cup	chopped flat-leaf parsley	125 mL
1/2 tsp	salt	2 mL
1/4 tsp	freshly ground black pepper	1 mL
	Fresh lemon wedges (optional)	

1. In a large skillet, heat olive oil over medium heat. Add garlic and cook for 1 minute or until softened. Do not allow to brown. Add chicken pieces; cook until browned on all sides.

2. Add wine and vinegar; increase heat slightly and bring to a gentle boil. Cook for about 5 minutes. Add whole and chopped olives, parsley, salt and pepper. Stir until well mixed.

3. Reduce heat, cover and simmer for 20 to 30 minutes, periodically turning chicken to make sure it cooks thoroughly. Add a splash of water or wine if chicken looks too dry.

4. Arrange chicken pieces on a warm serving platter and pour sauce over. Serve with fresh lemon wedges if desired.

Wine writer Michael Vaughan tells me that whenever he visits Italy, this dish is the first thing he orders. Once you taste it you'll know why.

When I make this dish, I take Michael's advice and use a kitchen mallet to crack the bones of the chicken. This encourages them to release their flavorful marrow; it also helps to flatten the chicken somewhat, making for a quicker cooking time.

There is something so good about this roast chicken – with its rub-down of olive oil, dried chilies, coarse salt, lots of cracked pepper and squirt of lemon – that I find myself continuing to think about it days after I enjoyed it. It's completely addictive. The only cure is to make it again.

Take care not to overcook the chicken or the white meat will become dry.

This dish is even more phenomenal when grilled over charcoal.

Pollo alla Diavola

Chicken with Chilies

1	roasting chicken (about 4 lbs [2 kg]), fat trimmed and cut down the back, allowing it to lie flat	1
3 tbsp	extra virgin olive oil	45 mL
1/2 tsp	salt	2 mL
1/4 tsp	freshly cracked black peppercorns	1 mL
2 tsp	red pepper flakes	10 mL
	Juice of 1 large lemon	

1. Place chicken skin-side up in an ovenproof dish, preferably terra cotta. Rub all over with olive oil, salt and cracked peppercorns; sprinkle with pepper flakes. Pour lemon juice over chicken, cover with plastic wrap and leave it to sit for at least 1 hour.

2. Preheat oven to 400° F (200° C). Roast chicken for about 60 to 65 minutes or until golden brown and crispy. If the skin begins to brown too quickly, reduce heat. Serve while very hot.

Spezzatino sounds so much more interesting than its English equivalent, "light stew." Indeed, translation does no justice at all to such a colorful, flavorful dish.

Vary the colors of the peppers if you wish; be warned, however, that green peppers do not "stew" as pleasantly as the yellow, orange or red varieties.

Spezzatino di Pollo con Peperoni

Stewed Chicken with Peppers

1 cup	dry white wine	250 mL
3	cloves garlic, peeled and smashed	3
3 tbsp	olive oil	45 mL
3	large yellow bell peppers, roasted, peeled and cut into strips	3
1	chicken (about 4 lbs [2 kg]), fat trimmed and cut into parts *or* equivalent weight of pre-cut chicken pieces	1
1	small onion, finely chopped	1
1 1/4 cups	*passata* (puréed, sieved tomatoes) *or* canned ground or crushed tomatoes	300 mL
	Salt and freshly ground black pepper to taste	
2 tbsp	chopped basil	25 mL

1. In a small bowl, combine wine and garlic; cover and let stand for at least 1 hour.

2. In a skillet heat a little of the olive oil over medium heat. Add pepper strips and a pinch of salt; cook 5 minutes or until tender. Transfer to a plate and set aside.

3. Add remaining oil to the skillet; cook chicken until browned on both sides. Reduce heat and continue to "dry cook" the chicken, partially covered, for about 25 to 30 minutes, turning the pieces occasionally. Transfer cooked chicken pieces to a serving platter and keep warm.

4. Increase heat slightly; add onion and cook 5 minutes or until softened. Add three-quarters of the reserved wine/garlic; bring to a boil and cook 6 minutes or until reduced and thickened slightly.

5. Add *passata* and basil, remaining wine and garlic, salt and pepper; cook for another 5 minutes, adding reserved peppers in the last minute. Pour mixture carefully over chicken pieces and serve immediately.

SERVES 4 TO 6

This lovely combination of chicken, sun-dried tomatoes and cheese originates from the region known as "The Marches" where, among other regional foods, wonderful Pecorino Romano is celebrated.

Pollo con Pomodori Secchi

Chicken with Sun-Dried Tomatoes

PREHEAT OVEN TO 375° F (190° C)

10	sun-dried tomatoes packed in oil, drained and cut into thin strips	10
2 cups	grated Pecorino Romano	500 mL
3 tbsp	butter	45 mL
6	boneless, skinless chicken breasts, opened, halved and pounded flat	6
1/4 cup	all-purpose flour	50 mL
1/4 cup	olive oil	50 mL
1 cup	dry white wine	250 mL
2	sprigs thyme	2
	Salt and freshly ground black pepper to taste	
1/4 cup	chopped flat-leaf parsley	50 mL

1. In a small bowl, mix together sun-dried tomatoes and cheese. Add butter and blend to form a paste. Set aside.

2. Arrange flattened chicken breasts on a clean work surface. If necessary, trim to a uniform shape and size. Distribute tomato/cheese mixture evenly between chicken pieces. Roll up each and secure with kitchen string. Dust with a little flour, shaking off excess.

3. In an ovenproof pan or skillet, heat the olive oil over high heat. Add chicken rolls and cook until browned on all sides. Transfer pan to preheated oven to cook for about 10 to 15 minutes, turning rolls over once or twice.

4. Carefully snip kitchen string and discard. Transfer chicken rolls to a serving platter and keep warm. Wearing oven mitts, return pan to the stovetop over medium-high heat. Add wine, thyme, salt and pepper; bring to a boil and cook for 10 minutes.

5. Remove thyme sprigs and adjust seasoning. Pour sauce over chicken, sprinkle with chopped parsley and serve immediately.

SERVES 4 TO 6

Here is a thoroughly delicious method of roasting chicken with an uncomplicated, yet unusual, fennel and potato stuffing and lots of soft, nutty baked garlic as an accompaniment.

Pollo alla Umbria

Umbrian-Style Chicken

PREHEAT OVEN TO 450° F (230° C)

1/4 cup	extra virgin olive oil	50 mL
1	onion, diced	1
2	heads garlic, separated and peeled; 2 cloves chopped	2
3	potatoes, peeled and cut into 1/2-inch (1 cm) cubes	3
1	small fennel bulb, trimmed, diced	1
1/2 tsp	salt	2 mL
1/4 tsp	freshly ground black pepper	1 mL
1/4 cup	fresh lemon juice	50 mL
1	roasting chicken, (about 4 1/2 lbs [2.25 kg])	1
2	branches rosemary	2
1 cup	dry white wine	250 mL

1. In a skillet heat 2 tbsp (25 mL) of the olive oil over medium-high heat. Add onion and cook for 5 minutes or until softened.

2. Add the chopped garlic, potatoes, fennel and 1/2 cup (125 mL) water; cook for 10 minutes or until potatoes are just tender. Season with salt, pepper and lemon juice. Remove from heat and allow stuffing to cool. Spoon stuffing into the chicken.

3. Rub chicken with 1 tbsp (15 mL) olive oil and additional salt and pepper. Set chicken breast-side down in a roasting pan; roast in preheated oven for 40 minutes. Turn chicken over (breast-side up) and surround evenly with whole garlic cloves and rosemary.

4. Drizzle 1 tbsp (15 mL) olive oil over garlic cloves; add 1 tbsp (15 mL) of the white wine. Roast for another 20 to 30 minutes or until juices run clear when chicken leg is pierced with a knife and garlic cloves are soft. Remove chicken from oven and transfer to a warmed serving platter; allow to rest for at least 15 minutes. Arrange garlic cloves around it. Spoon off most of the excess fat from the roasting pan and place pan over medium-high heat on top of the stove.

5. Add wine to pan, along with 1 cup (250 mL) water. Bring to a boil and cook for about 10 to 15 minutes, scraping up any bits from the bottom of the pan. When mixture has thickened slightly, pour into a warmed jug or gravy boat. Spoon out stuffing and cut chicken into 8 pieces. Serve with sauce.

Pollo con le Bietole

Chicken and Swiss Chard

3 tbsp	olive oil	45 mL
1	onion, chopped	1
2	carrots, scraped and finely chopped	2
1	stalk celery, chopped	1
4	cloves garlic, peeled and smashed	4
1	chicken, (about 4 1/2 lbs [2.25 kg]), cut into pieces *or* equivalent weight of pre-cut chicken pieces	1
1 cup	dry white wine	250 mL
1/2 cup	chicken stock	125 mL
1/2 tsp	salt	2 mL
1/4 tsp	freshly ground black pepper	1 mL
2 lbs	Swiss chard, washed, trimmed and chopped	1 kg
1 cup	whipping (35%) cream	250 mL

1. In a large skillet or Dutch oven, heat olive oil over medium heat. Add onion, carrot and celery; cook 5 minutes or until softened. Add garlic and cook until softened but not brown.

2. Add chicken, in batches if necessary, and brown on all sides. With all chicken in skillet, add wine and stock; increase heat slightly, bring to a gentle boil and cook for about 5 minutes. Add salt and pepper; mix well.

3. Reduce heat, cover and simmer for 20 to 30 minutes, turning chicken occasionally to make sure it cooks thoroughly. If it gets too dry, add a little more water or wine.

4. Add Swiss chard, nestling it beneath and around chicken pieces. Cook for 5 minutes or until Swiss chard is wilted. Add cream and bring to a boil; cook for about 5 minutes or until sauce thickens. Serve chicken with sauce poured over.

PESCI E FRUTTI DI MARE
FISH & SEAFOOD

Serves 6

In this interesting recipe, delicate sole fillets are quickly fried in olive oil and treated to a spice-infused white wine marinade for a couple of days. Traditionally served on the third Sunday in July to commemorate the Feast of the Holy Redeemer, the dish has origins that date from the 14th century.

Be sure to serve at room temperature.

This makes a lovely light supper on a hot summer day.

Sogliole in Saor

Venetian Sole

8-INCH (2 L) SQUARE BAKING DISH

1 lb	sole or flounder fillets	500 g
	Salt and freshly ground black pepper	
1/4 cup	all-purpose flour	50 mL
1/4 cup	olive oil (approximate)	50 mL
2	onions, thinly sliced	2
1 cup	dry white wine	250 mL
1 cup	wine vinegar (white or red)	250 mL
2	bay leaves	2
2	whole cloves, cracked	2
1/4 tsp	cinnamon	1 mL
1/3 cup	golden raisins	75 mL
3 tbsp	toasted pine nuts	45 mL
	Chopped parsley (optional)	

1. Season fish with salt and pepper; dip in flour to coat, and shake off excess. In a large nonstick skillet, heat 1/4 cup (50 mL) olive oil over medium-high heat; in batches, cook fish fillets for 5 minutes, turning once, or until golden brown. Drain on paper towel.

2. With a slotted spoon, remove any bits of fish or flour from the skillet. Add a little more oil (or drain excess) so that you have 1 tbsp (15 mL) oil in skillet. Reduce heat to medium; add onions and cook for 5 minutes or until golden and soft. Add wine, wine vinegar, bay leaves, cloves and cinnamon; bring to a boil, reduce heat to simmer and cook for 5 minutes.

3. Arrange fish in single layer in baking dish; sprinkle
    with salt and pepper. Pour hot marinade over fish and
    let cool to room temperature. Sprinkle with raisins
    and pine nuts, cover with plastic wrap and marinate
    in refrigerator for 1 to 2 days. Serve at room tempera-
    ture, sprinkled with chopped parsley, if desired.

SERVES 6

A thoroughly enjoyable combination favored by Chef Massimo Capra – and by me too! "People don't think of putting beans and shrimp together but it is very traditional and delicious," says the chef. A lovely addition to an antipasto spread, it also makes a wonderfully light first course. Serve with good crusty Italian bread to mop up the rich juices.

It is important that the beans are hot when combined with the other ingredients so they will absorb all the flavors.

Gamberi e Fagioli alla Massimo

Massimo's Shrimp and Beans

1 lb	dried romano beans, soaked overnight in water to cover	500 g
1	large red onion, thinly sliced	1
3	cloves garlic, minced	3
3/4 cup	lemon juice	175 mL
1/4 cup	extra virgin olive oil	50 mL
	Salt and freshly ground black pepper	
6 tbsp	butter	90 mL
2 lbs	medium shrimp (fresh or thawed from frozen), peeled and deveined	1 kg
3	large ripe plum tomatoes, diced	3
1 cup	chopped flat-leaf parsley	250 mL
1	bunch *frisée or* other salad greens, washed and trimmed	1

1. In a large saucepan, combine drained beans with cold water to cover by 2 inches (5 cm). Bring to a boil, reduce heat to simmer and cook 1 1/2 hours or until beans are tender. Drain.

2. In a bowl stir together hot beans, red onion, half the garlic, half the lemon juice and olive oil. Season to taste with salt and pepper. Cover with plastic wrap and keep in a warm place.

3. In a large skillet, melt butter over medium-high heat. Add shrimp, remaining garlic and remaining lemon juice; cook, stirring often, for 5 minutes or until shrimp are pink. Season to taste with salt and pepper.

4. Stir tomatoes and parsley into warm bean mixture. Pour onto a large serving platter; top with shrimp and their pan juices. Arrange *frisée* around edges and serve immediately.

SERVES 6

Here's a dish that shows why tuna is the definitive steak of the sea. And, as with its bovine counterpart, the most important thing here is not to overcook it.

While tuna is the traditional fish for this dish, you can substitute swordfish or even salmon steaks.

Tonno al Vino Rosso

Tuna in Red Wine

6	tuna steaks, cut 1/2 inch (1 cm) thick (about 2 1/2 lbs [1.25 kg] in total)	6
	Salt	
1/3 cup	all-purpose flour	75 mL
3 tbsp	olive oil	45 mL
2	cloves garlic, minced	2
1	large white onion, thinly sliced	1
1 1/2 cups	red wine	375 mL
3 tbsp	black peppercorns, cracked	45 mL
2 tbsp	chopped flat-leaf parsley	25 mL

1. Sprinkle tuna steaks with a little salt; dip in flour to coat and shake off excess.

2. In a large skillet, heat 1 tbsp (15 mL) of the oil over medium heat. Add garlic and onion; cook 5 minutes or until softened. With a slotted spoon, transfer onion mixture to a bowl.

3. Add remaining oil to skillet. In batches, cook the tuna steaks for 3 minutes per side. Return all tuna steaks to skillet, along with red wine, peppercorns, a pinch of salt and the onion mixture. Reduce heat to medium-low; cook for 5 minutes, turning fish once. Transfer to a warm serving platter. Sprinkle with parsley and serve immediately.

If you want to start an argument in the region known as Le Marche (The Marches) bring up the topic of brodetto.

As with many beloved Italian preparations, this rich fish stew has variations from one part of the province to the other. With all due respect to all those who have come before, I humbly present this very reputable version of an ancient, classic dish. I first experienced brodetto *far from The Marches, down in the southern seaport town of Monópoli, with fish and shellfish harvested only an hour before they met the pot.*

Plan to make the fish stock early in the day. Ask the fishmonger for a good assortment of non-oily fish heads, bones, bits and pieces to equal about 2 lbs (1 kg). Put all of it into your biggest stockpot. You can also add shells and any trimmings from the fish used in this recipe. Roughly cut an onion (skin and all), an unpeeled lemon, a carrot and a celery stalk; add along with a handful of black peppercorns, a few smashed garlic cloves, a good grinding of salt, a couple of bay leaves and sprigs of fresh thyme and parsley.

(Continued next page ...)

Brodetto

Fish Stew

1/3 cup	olive oil	75 mL
1	large onion, thinly sliced	1
	A few threads saffron	
	Salt and freshly ground black pepper	
4	cloves garlic, finely chopped	4
8 cups	hot fish stock (see instructions, lower left)	2 L
1 cup	dry white wine	250 mL
1	can (28 oz [796 mL]) Italian plum tomatoes, roughly chopped, plus 1/3 cup (75 mL) of their juice	1
3 lbs	assorted fish (such as monkfish, halibut, red snapper, red mullet, sea bass or cod fillets), cut into large chunks	1.5 kg
8 oz	mussels or clams, scrubbed and debearded; discard any with damaged shells	250 g
8 oz	large shrimp (fresh or thawed from frozen), peeled and deveined	250 g
1/4 cup	chopped flat-leaf parsley	50 mL
8	thick slices rustic country-style bread, brushed with oil, oven-toasted	8

1. In a large soup pot, heat olive oil over medium heat. Add onion, saffron and a pinch each of salt and pepper; cook for 5 minutes or until onion is softened. Stir in garlic; cook 1 minute longer. Do not allow garlic to brown.

2. Stir in fish stock, wine, tomatoes and their juice. Increase heat and boil for 1 minute. Reduce heat to simmer and cook for 15 minutes.

(Continued from page 146)

Cover with cold water (at least 10 cups [2.5 L]) and bring to a boil; lower heat and let it bubble away for no longer than 30 minutes, skimming the foam that will occasionally rise to the surface. Strain through a fine sieve and discard solids. Pour into a clean saucepan and keep hot over low heat. This is also a very good stock for seafood risottos.

3. Add fish chunks; cook another 5 minutes, increasing heat as necessary to maintain a gentle simmer. Add mussels and shrimp; cover and cook 2 minutes longer or until shellfish open and shrimp turns pink. (Discard any mussels or clams that do not open.) Stir in chopped parsley. Season to taste with salt and pepper. Put a toast in the bottom of each bowl; ladle soup over and serve immediately.

SERVES 4 TO 6

Here's a recipe from Chef Chris McDonald of Avalon restaurant in Toronto, who says of this dish (a staple on Avalon's menu): "this is a recipe dating from the 14th century that is traditionally served on Redeemer Day (Redentore) in Venice, the third Sunday in July." At Avalon, the marinated sardines are cooked on a wood-fired grill but they can also be pan-fried.

Sardine in Saor Avalon

Soused and Wood-Grilled Sardines Avalon

PREHEAT GRILL, IF USING

2 lbs	gutted and scaled sardines (heads intact), fresh or thawed from frozen	1 kg
	Olive oil for frying	
	All-purpose flour	
1/2 cup	extra virgin olive oil	125 mL
2	onions, thinly sliced	2
1 cup	white wine vinegar	250 mL
1 cup	dry white wine	250 mL
2 tbsp	pine nuts	25 mL
2 tbsp	currants, soaked in hot water, drained and patted dry	25 mL
1 tbsp	granulated sugar	15 mL
1/2 tsp	salt	2 mL
1/4 tsp	freshly ground black pepper	1 mL

1. Rinse and drain fish; pat dry with paper towel. Brush sardines with olive oil and place on preheated grill over medium-high heat. Cook 1 1/2 minutes per side or until cooked through. Place in glass or ceramic dish. (Alternatively, in a large skillet, heat 1/2 inch [1 cm] olive oil over medium-high heat; a few at a time, toss the fish in the flour, shake off excess and fry for 3 minutes or until golden brown and cooked through. Do not overcrowd. Drain on paper towel. Place on glass or ceramic dish.)

2. In a skillet, heat 1/2 cup (125 mL) extra virgin olive oil over medium heat. Add onions and cook 7 minutes or until tender. Stir in vinegar, wine, pine nuts, currants, sugar, salt and pepper. Increase heat and boil for 3 minutes. Pour over sardines; cool to room temperature. Cover with plastic wrap. Allow to marinate, refrigerated, for up to 5 days. Serve at room temperature.

Andrew Milne Allan of Zucca Trattoria kindly gave me this very old recipe which originated with Neapolitan fishermen. As the chef notes, "this is a recipe to use in the summer when the sweet taste of tomatoes and basil are at their peak and clean, uncomplicated flavors, and minimum fuss at the stove are what you are looking for. Obviously all the ingredients must be ottimi *– first rate."
(By the way, "mad water" refers to the quick and furious boil to which the fish is treated.)*

Finally, a suggested variation from the chef: "If you have a large portobello mushroom or two, they make a nice addition. Cut into thick slices, sauté quickly in a little olive oil and chopped garlic and add to the pan with the fish."

Pesce all'Acqua Pazza

Fish in Mad Water

1/4 cup	olive oil	50 mL
1	large clove garlic, thinly sliced	1
2	ripe tomatoes, peeled and thickly sliced	2
	Salt and freshly ground black pepper	
4	fish fillets (each 6 to 8 oz [175 to 250 g]), such as sea bass, grouper or salmon	4
8	whole basil leaves	8

1. In a large skillet, heat olive oil over medium-low heat. Add garlic and cook for 3 minutes or until just beginning to brown. Sprinkle tomato slices with salt and add to skillet; cook, shaking the pan occasionally, for 4 minutes or until tomatoes are warmed through and their juices start to run.

2. Add fish fillets along with 1 cup (250 mL) water; bring to a boil. Reduce heat to medium-high, cover and cook, turning once, for 4 minutes or until fish is cooked through. Lift fish onto serving plates. Season sauce with salt and pepper; pour over fish. Garnish with basil and serve immediately.

Teglia di Pesce al Forno

Baked Swordfish

PREHEAT OVEN TO 375° F (190° C)
13- BY 9-INCH (3 L) BAKING DISH, OILED

6	swordfish steaks, about 2 1/2 lbs (1.25 kg) in total	6
	Salt and freshly ground black pepper	
2 lbs	potatoes (about 6), peeled and thinly sliced	1 kg
1	large white onion, thinly sliced	1
1/4 cup	extra virgin olive oil	50 mL
1/4 cup	chopped flat-leaf parsley	50 mL
3	cloves garlic, finely chopped	3
1 or 2	dried chili peppers, crumbled	1 or 2

1. Season fish with salt and pepper on both sides. Distribute half of the potatoes and onion over bottom of prepared baking dish; season with salt and pepper. Lay fish steaks on top in a single layer. Drizzle half of the olive oil over the fish.

2. Evenly scatter parsley, garlic and chili peppers over the fish. Top with remaining potatoes and onions; season with salt and pepper. Drizzle with remaining olive oil.

3. Cover dish with foil. Bake for 45 minutes. Remove foil; bake 15 minutes longer or until potatoes are tender and fish is cooked through.

Cozze Gratinate

Baked Mussels

PREHEAT OVEN TO 400°F (200° C)
4-CUP (1 L) SHALLOW GRATIN DISH, GREASED

3 lbs	mussels, scrubbed and debearded	1.5 kg
3/4 cup	dry white wine	175 mL
1/2 cup	dry bread crumbs, lightly toasted	125 mL
1/4 cup	chopped flat-leaf parsley *or* oregano	50 mL
1 tbsp	coarsely grated lemon zest	15 mL
4	cloves garlic, finely chopped	4
	Salt and freshly ground black pepper	
1/4 cup	extra virgin olive oil	50 mL

1. In a large saucepan, combine mussels and wine. Cover and place over high heat. Cook for 5 minutes, shaking the pan or until mussels open. Remove from heat. (Discard any mussels that do not open.) Discard cooking liquid.

2. When cool enough to handle, pull mussels from their shells; place in prepared gratin dish. In a bowl, stir together bread crumbs, parsley, lemon zest and garlic; season to taste with salt and pepper and sprinkle over mussels. Drizzle olive oil evenly over mussels.

3. Bake for 10 minutes or until golden brown. Serve immediately.

In Sardinia, they like to cook whole fresh triglie (red mullet) with Vernaccia – a crisp white wine with an attractive, slightly bitter finish – but any full-bodied dry white wine will do nicely here. This dish can also be made with red snapper. In Italy, the head and tail are left intact to enhance the overall flavor of the dish, but they are by no means essential.

Pesce al Vino Bianco

Fish in White Wine

1/2 cup	olive oil	125 mL
1/4 cup	chopped flat-leaf parsley	50 mL
2	cloves garlic, finely chopped	2
1 lb	plum tomatoes, peeled and chopped *or* 4 cups (1 L) canned plum tomatoes, drained and chopped	500 g
1 tbsp	coarsely grated lemon zest	15 mL
1	whole red mullet *or* red snapper (about 2 lbs [1 kg]) scaled, gutted and rinsed	1
	Salt and freshly ground black pepper	
1 cup	dry white wine	250 mL
	Lemon wedges	

1. In a large skillet, heat olive oil over low heat. Add parsley and garlic; cook for 2 minutes. Stir in tomatoes and lemon zest, increase heat to medium and cook, stirring occasionally, for 10 minutes or until slightly thickened.

2. Lay the fish in the sauce; sprinkle with salt and pepper. Reduce heat to medium-low. Cook 10 minutes; turn fish and cook 6 to 10 minutes longer or until cooked through.

3. Transfer fish to a warm serving platter. Add wine to the sauce in the skillet; increase heat and boil for 1 minute. Season to taste with salt and pepper; pour over fish. Serve immediately with lemon wedges.

Verdura
Vegetables

Within this simple preparation resides the essence of rustic Italian cooking: startlingly fresh ingredients, simply paired and quickly put together. It has color, an easy style, incredible flavor and a wonderful history. If you make no other recipe from this book make this one – you will be astonished at just how good it is. Include lots of earthy, rustic country-style bread alongside to mop up the juices.

Don't choose overly huge peppers for this dish. While yellow or orange peppers can be used, green peppers just don't have the requisite depth of flavor.

In Piedmont they seem to have a penchant for stuffing. Besides peppers, they stuff onions with a sweet and savory filling that includes raisins, cheese and eggs. Mushrooms are filled with their own chopped stems combined with parsley, onions, anchovies and bread crumbs. Perhaps best of all, fresh peach halves are treated to a heavenly filling of crushed macaroons blended with egg, butter and sugar before being baked.

Peperoni alla Piemontese

Piedmont Peppers

13- BY 9-INCH (3 L) BAKING DISH, OILED
PREHEAT OVEN TO 350° F (180° C)

6	red bell peppers, halved and seeded, stems left intact	6
6	plum tomatoes, peeled and quartered	6
12	anchovy fillets, rinsed and roughly chopped	6
4	cloves garlic, thinly sliced	4
1/2 cup	extra virgin olive oil	125 mL
	Salt and freshly ground black pepper	
12	whole leaves flat-leaf parsley	12

1. Lay peppers in prepared baking dish, cut-side up, in one layer. Into each pepper cavity, place two pieces of tomato. Sprinkle with chopped anchovies, making sure each pepper gets the equivalent of a whole anchovy fillet. Evenly distribute the sliced garlic among the peppers. Carefully pour the olive oil over the peppers. Sprinkle with just a little bit of salt (because of anchovies) and lots of freshly ground black pepper.

2. Roast in the top half of preheated oven for 1 hour or until the peppers are tender. Cool slightly. Serve warm, garnished with parsley leaves.

Fagioli alla Toscana

White Beans with Tomato

PREHEAT OVEN TO 375° F (190° C)
8-CUP (2 L) CASSEROLE WITH LID

1/4 cup	olive oil	50 mL
1/4 cup	chopped flat-leaf parsley	50 mL
8	fresh sage leaves	8
2	branches rosemary	2
4	cloves garlic, finely chopped	4
1 cup	canned Italian plum tomatoes, chopped, with juices	250 mL
	Salt and freshly ground black pepper	
2 cups	dried *cannellini* (white kidney beans) *or* navy beans, soaked overnight in water to cover	500 mL
1 cup	grated Pecorino Romano	250 mL

SERVES 4 TO 6

Turn leftovers into a fabulous soup the day after enjoying these flavorful Tuscan-style baked beans scented with fresh rosemary and enriched with Pecorino Romano.

1. In a large skillet, heat olive oil over medium-low heat. Add parsley, sage, rosemary and garlic; cook, stirring occasionally, for 6 minutes or until the garlic is softened and the herbs are fragrant. Stir in tomatoes with juice and a pinch each of salt and pepper; cook for 3 minutes or until slightly thickened.

2. In casserole dish, stir together tomato mixture, drained beans and half of the Pecorino Romano. Add enough cold water to cover beans; stir well. Cover casserole and bake for 2 1/2 hours or until beans are tender, testing for doneness every 30 minutes. (Cooking time will depend on freshness of the beans.)

3. Remove and discard rosemary branches, which should be bare. Sprinkle remaining cheese over the surface. Cook, uncovered, for 10 minutes longer or until cheese is golden. Serve from casserole.

My daughter makes this wonderful potato salad throughout the summer and – no matter how hot the day – prefers to bake the potatoes whole before combining them, while warm, with the other ingredients. It is astonishingly good. You will have good results whether you boil or roast the potatoes.

If the amount of garlic is too intense for your taste, reduce by half.

Alysa's Patate alla Rustiche

Alysa's Rustic Potato Salad

2 lbs	red potatoes (about 8), scrubbed	1 kg
1/4 cup	extra virgin olive oil	50 mL
1/4 cup	chopped fresh mint	50 mL
2 tbsp	chopped flat-leaf parsley	25 mL
4	cloves garlic, minced	4
	Salt and freshly ground black pepper	

1. In a large saucepan, combine potatoes with lightly salted cold water to cover. Bring to a boil; reduce heat and cook until tender when pierced with the tip of a sharp knife. Drain.
2. When cool enough to handle, cut potatoes into bite-sized chunks. In a large bowl, combine potatoes, oil, mint, parsley, garlic and salt and pepper to taste. Let stand 30 minutes to let flavors develop. Serve barely warm or at room temperature.

In Italy, this salad is prepared in May when the fava (broad) beans are only just formed and still dozing in their lovely fuzz-lined pods. They are enjoyed uncooked, treated to the very best extra virgin olive oil and then paired with small cubes of young Pecorino. If you cannot find a young version of this sheep's milk cheese, substitute Emmental or even a mild Cheddar. The quantity of fresh beans may seem like a lot, but remember they are still in the pod, which adds to their weight. Use your very finest olive oil for this dish.

Insalata di Fave e Pecorino

Baby Fava Bean and Pecorino Salad

5 lbs	young fava beans (in pods)	2.5 kg
	Salt and freshly ground black pepper to taste	
1/4 cup	extra virgin olive oil	50 mL
12 oz	young Pecorino Romano, cut into neat 1/2-inch (1 cm) cubes	375 g

1. Pod the beans and place in a medium-size bowl. Season with salt and pepper. Add olive oil gradually and toss to make sure all beans are well coated. (The beans should not be floating in oil.)
2. Add cubes of cheese and toss once or twice. Serve at once with crusty bread to mop up the oil.

SERVES 4 TO 6

Delightfully easy, this dish is perfect as part of an al fresco summer spread.

Involtino di Melanzane

Eggplant Rolls with Cheese

2	eggplants (each about 1 lb [500 g])	2
2 tsp	coarse salt	10 mL
1/3 cup	all-purpose flour	75 mL
1/3 cup	olive oil	75 mL
1 1/2 cups	high-quality tomato sauce	375 mL
8 oz	Italian mozzarella, shredded	250 g
12	basil leaves	12
	Salt and freshly ground black pepper	
1/2 cup	grated Parmigiano-Reggiano	125 mL

1. Wash and trim each eggplant and cut lengthwise into 6 slices. Sprinkle with salt; place in a colander set in the sink to drain for 30 minutes. Rinse under cold running water. Pat dry with paper towels.

2. Spread flour out on a large plate. Dip eggplant slices in flour, shaking off the excess. In a large nonstick skillet, heat 1 tbsp (15 mL) of the olive oil over medium-high heat; cook 3 eggplant slices, turning once, 5 minutes or until golden and tender. Drain on paper towel. Repeat with remaining olive oil and eggplant slices.

3. Spread half of tomato sauce over bottom of prepared baking dish; set aside. Sprinkle shredded mozzarella evenly over eggplant slices. Put a basil leaf on each slice of eggplant and sprinkle with salt and pepper. Roll up each eggplant slice to form a neat package. Put rolls in baking dish, seam side down. Pour remaining tomato sauce over eggplant rolls.

4. Sprinkle with Parmigiano-Reggiano. Bake for 15 to 20 minutes or until cheese is melted and everything is heated through. Serve hot or warm.

Fave con Pancetta

Fava Beans with Bacon

1 tbsp	extra virgin olive oil	15 mL
4 oz	pancetta, diced	125 g
1	onion, thinly sliced	1
1	stalk celery, chopped	1
1 lb	shelled young fresh fava beans (about 3 lbs [1.5 kg] unshelled fava beans)	500 g
1 cup	beef stock	250 mL
	Salt and freshly ground black pepper	
2 tbsp	chopped flat-leaf parsley	25 mL

1. In a large skillet, heat olive oil over medium heat. Add pancetta, onion and celery; cook, stirring often, 8 minutes or until vegetables are softened.

2. Stir in fava beans and beef stock. Bring to a boil, reduce heat to medium-low and cook, uncovered, stirring occasionally, for 25 minutes or until beans are tender.

3. Season to taste with salt and pepper. Stir in parsley and serve immediately.

Finocchio Parmigiana

Fennel with Parmigiano-Reggiano Cheese

In Italy, every part of finocchio (fennel) is used. The leaves and stalks are used to make stuffings, while the seeds add their distinctive flavor to salamis and sausage. Young, crisp fennel bulbs are often eaten raw at the end of a meal in place of fruit or in simple salads with a vinaigrette. Or they can be enjoyed in the simple, appetizing manner presented here. Great with any fish.

PREHEAT OVEN TO 350° F (180° C)
12-CUP (3 L) GRATIN OR CASSEROLE DISH

4	fennel bulbs, trimmed, halved, cored and sliced	4
3 tbsp	extra virgin olive oil	45 mL
1/3 cup	dry bread crumbs	75 mL
2 tbsp	chopped flat-leaf parsley	25 mL
2	cloves garlic, finely chopped	2
1 cup	grated Parmigiano-Reggiano	250 mL
	Salt and freshly ground black pepper to taste	

1. In a large pot of boiling water, cook fennel for 5 minutes or until tender. Drain. Rinse under cold running water; drain again. Pat dry with paper towels; set aside.

2. Lightly brush gratin or casserole dish with a little of the olive oil. In a bowl stir together bread crumbs, parsley, garlic and half of the Parmigiano-Reggiano. Stir in fennel to coat evenly with the mixture. Season to taste with salt and pepper. Transfer to prepared dish.

3. Sprinkle with remaining cheese and drizzle with remaining oil. Bake for 15 minutes or until golden brown.

SERVES 4 TO 6

The best lentils for this dish are the little dark green ones called cavellucchi in Italy and puy *in France. They remain firm during cooking — unlike the conventional orange or pale green lentils, which become a little too mushy.*

Lenticchie in Umido

Lentils Cooked with Wine and Tomato

2 tbsp	olive oil	25 mL
2	cloves garlic, finely chopped	2
1	onion, finely chopped	1
1	carrot, finely chopped	1
1 1/2 cups	lentils (see note at left), soaked in cold water overnight	375 mL
1 cup	dry red wine	250 mL
1 cup	*passata* (puréed, sieved tomatoes) *or* canned ground plum tomatoes	250 mL
1 cup	chicken stock *or* vegetable stock	250 mL
1/2 tsp	salt	2 mL
1/4 tsp	freshly ground black pepper	1 mL
1 lb	spinach	500 g

1. In a large skillet, heat olive oil over medium-high heat. Add garlic, onion and carrot; cook, stirring occasionally, for 7 minutes or until vegetables are softened. Stir in drained lentils; cook 2 minutes longer.

2. Pour in wine. Bring to a boil; boil for 2 minutes. Reduce heat to medium-low. Stir in *passata*, stock, salt and pepper. Cover and cook, stirring occasionally, for 20 minutes or until lentils are tender. Meanwhile, prepare spinach.

3. Trim and wash spinach. Put the spinach in a large saucepan with just the water that clings to the leaves after washing. Cook, covered, over high heat until steam begins to escape from beneath lid. Remove lid, toss spinach and cook 1 minute longer or until tender. Remove from heat. Drain, pressing spinach against sides of colander to squeeze out as much water as possible. Chop spinach roughly. Set aside.

4. When lentils are tender, stir in spinach. Adjust seasoning as necessary and serve.

FAGIOLI ALLA TOSCANA • WHITE BEANS WITH TOMATO (PAGE 155) ➤

Here is a preparation that will put to good use all those baskets full of small zucchini your garden produces each summer.

High-quality back bacon cut into strips can replace pancetta.

This dish is very good with chicken, on its own, or tossed with your favorite pasta.

Zucchine con Pancetta

Zucchini with Bacon

12	small zucchini (about 3 lbs [1.5 kg])	12
1 tsp	salt	5 mL
1/2 lb	pancetta *or* back bacon, cut into thin strips	250 g
1	onion, sliced	1
3	cloves garlic, minced	3
2 tbsp	chopped flat-leaf parsley	25 mL
2 tbsp	chopped marjoram *or* oregano	25 mL
1 lb	plum tomatoes, peeled, seeded and chopped *or* 4 cups (1 L) canned plum tomatoes, seeded, drained and chopped	500 g
	Salt and freshly ground black pepper to taste	

1. Peel zucchini and slice into 1/4-inch (5 mm) rounds. Put in a colander set in the sink; sprinkle with salt. Let stand 1 hour. Rinse under cold running water. Pat dry with paper towels.

2. In a large skillet set over medium heat, cook pancetta and onion for 5 minutes or until onion is softened. Stir in garlic, parsley and marjoram; cook, stirring occasionally, for 10 minutes or until well browned.

3. Stir in tomatoes, zucchini, a pinch of salt and plenty of freshly ground black pepper. Cook, stirring occasionally, for 15 minutes or until zucchini is tender. Serve immediately.

◄ PERE AL FORNO • *BAKED PEARS* (PAGE 176)

This simple side dish requires the freshest walnuts – so buy them unshelled if available. To boost the flavor, briefly toast unchopped walnuts in the oven on a baking sheet; keep a careful eye on them, since they can burn quickly.

Indivia alle Noci e Pancetta

Endive with Walnuts and Pancetta

6-CUP (1.5 L) GRATIN DISH OR OTHER OVENPROOF DISH

3 tbsp	olive oil	45 mL
1/4 lb	pancetta, finely chopped	125 g
2	cloves garlic, finely chopped	2
6	Belgian endives, washed, trimmed and cut in half lengthwise	6
1/2 cup	dry white wine	125 mL
1/4 tsp	salt	1 mL
1/4 tsp	freshly ground black pepper	1 mL
1 cup	grated Parmigiano-Reggiano	250 mL
1 cup	walnut halves, chopped (reserve a few, unchopped, for garnish)	250 mL

1. In a large skillet, heat the olive oil over medium heat. Add pancetta and garlic; cook for 3 minutes. Do not let garlic brown. Add endives; cook for 3 minutes, turning once or twice with tongs. Arrange endives cut-side down. Pour in wine; sprinkle with salt and pepper. Cover skillet, reduce heat to medium-low and cook 10 minutes or until endives are tender. Preheat broiler.

2. Transfer cooked endives and skillet contents to gratin dish. Sprinkle with grated Parmigiano-Reggiano. Broil for 2 minutes or until cheese is lightly browned. Sprinkle with chopped walnuts. Serve immediately, garnished with halved walnuts.

Verzada e Patate

Savoy Cabbage with Potatoes

2 lbs	boiling potatoes, peeled and quartered	1 kg
2 lbs	Savoy cabbage, cored and coarsely chopped	1 kg
1/4 cup	olive oil	50 mL
1 tbsp	butter	15 mL
4	cloves garlic, minced	4
3 tbsp	chopped flat-leaf parsley	45 mL
	Salt and freshly ground black pepper	

1. Bring a large pot of lightly-salted water to a boil. Add potatoes; reduce heat to simmer and cook for 10 minutes or until potatoes are softened. (They should not be fully cooked.) Stir in cabbage; cook for 15 minutes longer or until potatoes and cabbage are tender. Drain.

2. Return drained vegetables to the pot. Cook over low heat for several minutes, shaking the pot, until residual moisture evaporates and potatoes and cabbage are relatively dry. Remove pot from heat and cover.

3. In a skillet, heat olive oil and butter over medium heat. Add garlic and cook for 2 minutes or until softened. Do not allow garlic to brown. Stir in parsley and immediately pour skillet contents over potatoes and cabbage, scraping with a rubber spatula to get all of mixture.

4. Roughly mash vegetables with the oil mixture. Season to taste with salt and pepper and serve immediately.

SERVES 4 TO 6

I had my first authentic Italian eating experience molti years ago in a cramped, jovial trattoria in London's Soho. It was the simplest of meals — yet so good, so real, I can still taste every component today: thin scaloppine di vitello al limone with lots of fresh chopped parsley was laid next to rounds of crispy pan-fried potato. Sharing plate space was a mound of deep, dark spinach, shiny with olive oil and flecked with bits of garlic, a wedge of lemon placed alongside.

I took the waiter's advice and squeezed the lemon onto it while he held aloft a pepper mill as long as a piano leg that rained fresh pepper over the glistening greens. I was an instant convert to the Italian way with vegetables. This method works well with Swiss chard, rapini, green beans or zucchini.

Spinaci Saltati al Limone

Sautéed Spinach with Lemon

3 lbs	fresh spinach	1.5 kg
3 tbsp	olive oil	45 mL
3	cloves garlic, finely chopped	3
	Salt and freshly ground black pepper to taste	
1	lemon, cut into wedges	1

1. Trim and wash spinach. Put the spinach in a large saucepan with just the water that clings to the leaves after washing. Cook, covered, over high heat until steam begins to escape from beneath lid. Remove lid, toss spinach and cook 1 minute longer or until tender. Remove from heat. Drain; return to pot. Cook over medium-high heat, shaking the pot, until moisture evaporates.

2. Add olive oil, garlic and salt and pepper to taste. Cook, stirring, for 2 minutes. Do not let garlic brown. Serve immediately, sprinkled with lemon juice and freshly ground black pepper.

I love this dish because it combines two of my favorite vegetables – potatoes and tomatoes – in one simple preparation.

The Italians create many wonderful potato dishes that can be enjoyed as a side dish or, as in this case, a light main course. Most can be prepared up to a day ahead and reheated before serving.

Plan to make this dish during late summer, when fresh plum tomatoes are plentiful.

If you're fussy and time is not an issue, peel the tomatoes with a vegetable peeler.

Tortino di Patate

Potato Gratin

PREHEAT OVEN TO 400° F (200° C)
13- BY 9-INCH (3 L) BAKING DISH, OILED

1/4 cup	extra virgin olive oil	50 mL
4 lbs	large baking potatoes (about 6), peeled and cut crosswise into thin slices	2 kg
2	onions, thinly sliced	2
1 lb	ripe firm plum tomatoes, seeded and diced	500 g
3	cloves garlic, finely chopped	3
4 tsp	chopped oregano	20 mL
1 tsp	salt	5 mL
1/2 tsp	freshly ground black pepper	2 mL
1 cup	grated Pecorino Romano	250 mL

1. In a large mixing bowl, combine 2 tbsp (25 mL) of the olive oil, potatoes, onions, tomatoes, garlic, oregano, salt, pepper and 1/2 cup (125 mL) of the Pecorino Romano. Use your hands to combine well.

2. Transfer the potato mixture into prepared baking dish. Drizzle with olive oil. Sprinkle with remaining Pecorino Romano.

3. Cover dish with foil. Bake for 45 minutes. Remove foil; bake 15 minutes longer or until potatoes are tender. Let stand for 15 minutes before serving.

SERVES 4 TO 6

SERVES 4 TO 6

In some parts of Italy, zucchini are filled with a savory meat stuffing. But I prefer this version from Liguria, which combines soft bread crumbs, cheese and dried mushrooms. Very nice on their own or treated to an uncomplicated tomato sauce.

Look for relatively small zucchini for this dish.

Eggplant and peppers may be cooked in the same fashion.

Be sure to use fresh marjoram; to my mind, dried marjoram bears little resemblance to the real thing.

Zucchine Ripiene

Stuffed Zucchini

PREHEAT OVEN TO 350° F (180° C)
13- BY 9-INCH (3 L) BAKING DISH, LIGHTLY GREASED

2 lbs	zucchini (about 4 medium), washed and trimmed	1 kg
1	day-old Italian bread roll, crusts removed	1
1/4 cup	milk	50 mL
3/4 cup	grated Parmigiano-Reggiano	175 mL
2 tsp	chopped fresh marjoram	10 mL
1/2 oz	dried porcini mushrooms, soaked, drained and finely chopped	15 g
	Salt and freshly ground black pepper	
2	eggs, lightly beaten	2
	Lemon wedges *or* tomato sauce	

1. In a large pot of lightly salted boiling water, cook whole zucchini for 5 minutes; drain. In a small bowl, combine roll and milk; set aside.

2. When cool enough to handle, cut zucchini in half lengthwise. Using a small spoon or melon baller, carefully scrape out the pulp, being careful not to split the sides of the zucchini. Chop pulp to a uniform consistency; put in a bowl. Place zucchini shells in prepared baking dish.

3. Squeeze bread of excess milk. Add bread to chopped zucchini pulp along with Parmigiano-Reggiano, marjoram and mushrooms; mix well. Season to taste with salt and pepper. Stir in eggs. Spoon mixture into zucchini shells, dividing it evenly.

4. Bake 30 minutes or until filling is set and zucchini is tender when pierced with the tip of a sharp knife. Serve hot, with a squeeze of lemon or with tomato sauce.

DOLCI
SWEET THINGS

A delightful cross between a flourless cake and a sumptuous rice pudding, this dessert is delicious served warm with fresh peeled, sliced peaches or a few pitted cherries.

To toast almonds, place on a baking sheet and bake at 350° F (180° C) for 10 to 15 minutes or until golden brown and fragrant.

Torta di Budino di Riso

Rice Pudding Cake

PREHEAT OVEN TO 325° F (160° C)
9-INCH (3 L) TUBE PAN, BUTTERED

4 1/2 cups	2% milk	1.125 L
1 cup	short-grain Italian Arborio rice	250 mL
1 cup	granulated sugar	250 mL
1/2 cup	blanched, slivered almonds, toasted and chopped	125 mL
2 tbsp	grated lemon zest	25 mL
1 tsp	vanilla extract	5 mL
4	eggs, separated	4
2 tbsp	dry bread crumbs	25 mL
	Icing sugar	

1. In a large, heavy saucepan, bring milk to a boil over medium-high heat. Add rice, stir once and return to a boil. Immediately reduce heat to low and simmer until mixture is thick and creamy, about 20 minutes, stirring occasionally to prevent sticking.

2. Add half of the sugar, stir and cook for another 2 to 3 minutes. Remove from heat and let cool.

3. Stir the chopped almonds, lemon zest, vanilla extract, egg yolks and remaining sugar into rice-milk mixture, blending well. Allow to cool thoroughly.

4. Sprinkle bread crumbs over bottom of prepared tube pan, shaking off excess. In a clean, deep mixing bowl, beat egg whites with a pinch of salt until stiff peaks form. Using a rubber spatula, gently fold egg whites into the rice mixture. Pour into tube pan and bake for about 1 hour or until cake is light golden and puffed.

5. Cool completely in the pan before transferring to serving plate. Sift a little icing sugar over before cutting into wedges and serving.

Pesche con Mascarpone

Peaches with Mascarpone

SERVES 4 TO 6

Fresh peaches and crumbled amaretti *are a classic combination. Fill the peach cavities first with luxurious mascarpone cheese and a good thing becomes great — seductive, even. A more formal version can be prepared by gently poaching the fresh peaches in a not-too-dry white wine before filling. Or try brushing fresh peach halves with a mixture of brown sugar and water, then grilling them.*

Look for amaretti *in Italian grocery stores.*

1 1/2 cups	mascarpone cheese	375 mL
1/4 cup	whipping (35%) cream	50 mL
6	ripe peaches, cut in half, pitted (if skin is particularly fuzzy or tough, blanch peaches in boiling water, refresh in cold water and peel)	6
16	*amaretti* (Italian macaroon-type biscuits), crumbled	16

1. In a mixing bowl, blend cheese and cream together until smooth.

2. Spoon mixture into each peach half. Top with crumbled *amaretti* and serve.

SERVES 6 TO 8

Make this classic chocolate sweet the night before so it has plenty of time to set. Cut it with a sharp knife dipped in hot water and wiped clean after every cut. Delicious with a little rum-spiked unsweetened whipped cream.

Make sure the eggs you use for this preparation are ultra-fresh.

Dolce al Cioccolato

Chilled Chocolate Log

8- BY 4-INCH (1.5 L) LOAF PAN, LINED WITH PLASTIC WRAP

8 oz	imported semisweet or bittersweet chocolate, chopped into small pieces	250 g
1/4 cup	dark rum	50 mL
1/2 cup	butter, softened	125 mL
2 tbsp	granulated sugar	25 mL
	Salt	
2	eggs, separated	2
1 1/2 cups	blanched almonds, finely chopped	375 mL
12	plain butter biscuits, broken into 1-inch (2.5 cm) pieces	12
	Icing sugar	

1. Melt the chocolate in a small saucepan placed inside a larger one filled with boiling water (be very careful not to allow any water to splash into the chocolate) or in a microwave. When completely melted, stir in rum. Chocolate will firm up and then loosen. Allow mixture to cool completely.

2. In a large bowl, cream together butter and sugar until light and fluffy. In another bowl, beat egg whites with a little salt until soft peaks form. Reserve.

3. Add egg yolks, one at a time, to butter mixture, beating well after each addition. Stir in chopped almonds and chocolate mixture. Gently fold beaten egg whites into the chocolate mixture until they all but disappear. Gently fold in the chopped biscuits, incorporating them well.

4. Spoon mixture into loaf pan, spreading the top smooth and evenly with a spatula. Cover with plastic wrap and refrigerate overnight.

5. Remove from refrigerator about an hour before serving. Loosen the loaf by running a small sharp knife around the edges.

6. Using the plastic wrap for handles, lift the loaf out of the pan and invert it onto serving platter. Dust with a little icing sugar and cut into thin slices with a sharp knife, wiped clean after each slice. Serve with whipped cream or a thinned custard sauce.

This is one of the ways they enjoy apples in Lombardy (and the way my Mum used to make fritters for my daughter Jenna, who now makes them for her little son, Colsen). Use Granny Smith apples for these little fritters, since they retain their firm quality best.

In Italy, I've had sweet fritters fried in a mild, light-tasting olive oil, but vegetable oil may also be used.

Try serving with mascarpone thinned and blended with a little whipping cream.

Mele Fritte Jenna

Apple Fritters Jenna

2 cups	all-purpose flour	500 mL
1	egg	1
1 1/4 cups	milk	300 mL
1 1/4 cups	water	300 mL
3	apples, peeled, cored and thinly sliced to make 48 wedges	3
	Olive oil *or* vegetable oil for frying (enough to cover battered apples as they cook)	
	Icing sugar or granulated sugar for dusting	

1. Place flour in a mixing bowl, making a well in the center. Add egg and whisk it into flour. Gradually whisk in milk and water to form a batter. Cover with plastic wrap and refrigerate for about 30 minutes before using.

2. Add apple slices to the batter, turning and tossing to coat them all evenly. Meanwhile, line a platter with paper towels.

3. In a deep heavy saucepan, add oil to a depth of 2 to 3 inches (5 to 7.5 cm); heat over medium-high heat to 375° F (190° C).

4. Working in batches, place coated apple slices in hot oil and fry, turning once or twice for about 3 minutes or until golden brown on both sides.

5. Remove with a slotted spoon to paper towel-lined platter. Sprinkle with sugar and serve immediately.

SERVES 4 TO 6

You would expect the province that produces balsamic vinegar – that dark elixir with so many magical properties – to invent dozens of unconventional ways to enjoy it. This refreshing combination works remarkably well and is just one of them. The lemon zest and mint are not traditional but I think they help to lift the flavors even higher.

Put everything together before you sit down to your first course to allow time for the flavors to develop.

Start off with the minimum of sugar and add more depending on the sweetness of the berries.

5 cups is about 1 quart.

Fragole al Balsamico

Strawberries with Balsamic Vinegar

5 cups	ripe strawberries, washed and hulled	1.25 L
3 tbsp	high-quality balsamic vinegar	45 mL
1 tbsp	grated lemon zest	15 mL
20 to 25	mint leaves, washed, dried and chopped	20 to 25
2 to 3 tbsp	extra-fine sugar	25 to 45 mL

1. Slice strawberries into thirds and place in mixing bowl. Add balsamic vinegar, mix well and allow to marinate for about 25 minutes.

2. Add lemon zest, mint and sugar; mix well and serve.

SERVES 6 TO 8

This literally translates as "cooked cream" – a humble (and somewhat misleading) description for such an elegant, utterly delicious sweet. I think of it more as "captured cream," with the gelatin acting as captor to lustrous thick cream. While today's flash chefs often like to pair it with a trendy berry coulis, I believe this is one lily that should remain ungilded.

I ordered this dessert at a lovely restaurant in Lecce, where I was enjoying dinner with a number of American food writers, none of whom had heard of it. It appeared, then disappeared as quickly as I invited them to try it. Before dinner was over, eight more servings had been dispatched to our table.

Panna Cotta

Cooked Cream Pudding

4 cups	whipping (35%) cream	1 L
3/4 cup	granulated sugar	175 mL
1 tsp	vanilla extract	5 mL
1	envelope gelatin	1

1. In a heavy saucepan over medium-low heat, warm cream, sugar and vanilla, just until cream is beginning to ripple a little. Reduce heat and simmer for 10 minutes.

2. In a small bowl, combine the gelatin and 1/4 cup (50 mL) boiling water and let sit for 1 minute. Add another 1/4 cup (50 mL) boiling water to gelatin; combine with hot cream. Stir to dissolve gelatin.

3. Pour mixture into ramekins or glass custard cups; cool and refrigerate for about 4 hours or up to 24 hours.

Torta di Noce

Walnut Cake

SERVES 6 TO 8

MAKES ABOUT
12 SLICES

Hazelnuts, almonds and walnuts are all used to flavor simple teacakes in Italy. This one, from Ristorante Paradiso in Caserta, Italy, is particularly good when thickly sliced and spread with a little butter. The fresher the walnuts, the better the cake, so buy nuts in the shell if they are available – 20 will be enough for this recipe.

PREHEAT OVEN TO 350° F (180° C)

8- BY 4-INCH (1.5 L) LOAF PAN, GREASED
(OR LINED WITH WAXED PAPER)

1/4 cup	butter, softened	50 mL
3/4 cup	granulated sugar	175 mL
1 tbsp	finely grated lemon zest	15 mL
	Juice of 1 lemon	
1	egg	1
1 1/2 cups	all-purpose flour	375 mL
1 1/2 tsp	baking powder	7 mL
1/2 cup	milk	125 mL
2 tbsp	golden raisins, soaked in hot water, drained and dried	25 mL
1 cup	whole walnuts, coarsely chopped	250 mL
1 tbsp	all-purpose flour	15 mL

1. In a bowl with a wooden spoon, cream butter and sugar together. Beat in lemon zest and juice. Beat in egg until fluffy.

2. In another bowl, stir together flour and baking powder. Stir into butter mixture, a little bit at a time, alternately with the milk, mixing well after each addition.

3. In the empty dry ingredient bowl, toss raisins and walnuts with the tablespoon (15 mL) of flour, then add to the batter, blending well.

4. Pour batter into prepared pan, banging down on work surface to settle the batter evenly. Bake in preheated oven for about 60 to 70 minutes or until a tester comes out clean. Cool on a rack before slicing.

As close to heaven as a sexy dessert can get. If you don't have a double boiler in which to make the sauce (or a zabaglione, as this particular one is referred to in Italy), improvise with one small saucepan set inside a larger one filled with hot (not boiling) water.

If you can find them, try this beautiful dish with ripe black figs split in half; no need to cook them beforehand.

Use the best fruits of the season: strawberries in spring, figs in late summer and pears in autumn and winter.

Pere al Forno

Baked Pears

PREHEAT BROILER

1 tsp	almond oil *or* walnut oil *or* any light-tasting oil	5 mL
12	small ripe pears, peeled, trimmed, seeded and quartered	12
4	egg yolks	4
1/4 cup	Marsala *or* dry sherry	50 mL
1/4 cup	sugar	50 mL

1. Brush a flat ceramic or glass baking dish with oil. Lay poached pears in dish.

2. In double boiler, or mixing bowl over a saucepan of hot (not boiling) water, whisk together egg yolks, Marsala and sugar for about 7 to 10 minutes or until doubled in volume, foamy and light.

3. Pour *zabaglione* over the pears and place under preheated hot broiler, for 1 to 2 minutes, or just until the top begins to brown in patches. (Be sure to watch it carefully.) Serve immediately.

SERVES 6 TO 8

For many years I chose to cele-brate my birthday at Il Posto, an elegant Italian restaurant in Toronto. One year, I spotted actor and bon vivant Peter Ustinov sitting at a corner table completing his solo supper with a plate of these beautiful caramelized oranges. Inspired by his choice, I followed suit. Now, I think of Peter Ustinov whenever I eat these delicious, refreshing oranges. If you can find blood oranges (called sanguinelli) – fruit of the gods, if there ever was one – I urge you to use them here.

Arance Caramellizzate

Caramelized Oranges

8	large seedless oranges, washed	8
1	lemon, juiced	1
1 cup	sugar	250 mL
1/4 cup	Grand Marnier *or* Cointreau	50 mL
	Fresh mint for garnish (optional)	

1. Halve and squeeze the juice from 1 of the oranges over a bowl and reserve. Remove zest from 2 of the oranges and cut into very thin (1/8-inch [3 mm]) shreds. Set aside. Peel all oranges and, with a sharp knife, remove and discard the white pith.

2. Carefully slice oranges crosswise into 1/4-inch (5 mm) slices. Place in a sieve over the reserved bowl to collect juice. Transfer juice with lemon juice to a small saucepan and heat gently over low heat.

3. In a deep heavy saucepan, heat sugar over low heat; do not stir but leave to turn a little dark at the edges. Slowly add warmed orange juice and lemon juice, orange zest and orange liqueur. (Be careful of spluttering.) Stir with a wooden spoon until the mixture becomes foamy and golden brown in color.

4. Place orange slices in the syrup and let sit for about 20 minutes. Transfer oranges and syrup to a serving dish, cover with plastic wrap and chill in the refrigerator for a few hours or overnight before serving. If desired, serve garnished with fresh mint.

Torta della Nonna

Pine Nut Cake

SERVES 6 TO 8

My good friend Leslie Fruman gave me a copy of Frances Mayes' lovely little book "Under The Tuscan Sun" to read, as she said, "for inspiration," while I was working on this book. Well, it worked... sort of. Now, I want to own and restore a rambling old house in Italy, and gather the pine cones that hold the pinoli to make this lovely traditional sweet – just as the author and thousands of Italian grandmothers did before her.

PREHEAT OVEN TO 400° F (200° C)

Custard filling

2 cups	milk	500 mL
1/2 cup	sugar	125 mL
	Zest of 1 lemon, cut into thin strips	
2	egg yolks	2
Pinch	salt	Pinch
1/3 cup	all-purpose flour	75 mL
1 1/2 tsp	vanilla extract	7 mL

Polenta pastry

1 1/2 cups	fine polenta	375 mL
1 1/2 cups	all-purpose flour	375 mL
1/3 cup	granulated sugar	75 mL
1 1/2 tsp	baking powder	7 mL
1/2 cup	butter, chilled	125 mL
1	egg	1
1	egg yolk	1

Topping

1 cup	pine nuts	250 mL

1. In a large, heavy saucepan, combine milk and half the sugar; slowly bring to a boil. Add lemon zest and whisk until blended.

2. In a bowl whisk together egg yolks, remaining sugar and salt until mixture is thick and golden colored. Whisk 1/3 cup (75 mL) flour into mixture; blend until smooth. Add 1/2 cup (125 mL) of the hot milk and sugar mixture; whisk together well.

3. Using a spatula, transfer the contents of the bowl to the remaining hot milk and sugar mixture in the saucepan and continue whisking over medium heat until thick, about 2 to 3 minutes. Bring to a gentle boil and keep whisking and stirring for 1 minute. Remove from heat and discard lemon zest. Stir in vanilla. Set aside to cool.

4. Polenta Pastry: In a bowl combine polenta, flour, sugar and baking powder; blend well with a fork. Cut in chilled butter in pieces, using your hands to blend until the ingredients resemble fine bread crumbs. Add the whole egg and the egg yolk. Blend together well using a fork until a dough forms.

5. Divide dough into 2 pieces — one a little larger than the other. Roll out each between 2 sheets of waxed paper. Use the large piece to fill the bottom of 9-inch (23 cm) pie plate and the smaller piece for the lid. Spoon custard into pastry-lined pie plate. Cover with lid. Flute edges to create a decorative seal.

6. With a sharp knife, cut 2 or 3 vents in the center of the pie to allow steam to escape. Cover the top of the pastry with the pine nuts. Bake in preheated oven for about 20 minutes; reduce heat to 350° F (180° C) and continue baking another 20 minutes or until pastry and pine nuts are golden brown. Let stand about 40 minutes before serving.

SERVES 6 TO 8

Pan di Spagna *literally translates as "Spanish bread" and (according to Nick Malgieri, pastry chef and teacher extraordinaire) is thought to refer to the time of the Spanish Bourbon rule in Naples. The sponge cake itself reminds me very much of the "Victoria sandwich" that my English-born Mum used to make. It was essentially the same no-butter sponge cake, split and spread with raspberry jam and fresh whipped cream and dusted with icing sugar.*

If you can't find potato flour (also called potato starch) use cornstarch.

This simple cake can be cut into wedges and served warm with fresh fruit, or with fresh-cracked nuts and Italian cheeses.

Pan di Spagna con le Prugne

Sponge Cake with Prunes

PREHEAT OVEN TO 350° F (180° C)
9-INCH (23 CM) SPRINGFORM PAN LINED WITH
PARCHMENT PAPER

Topping

1 1/2 tbsp	sugar	20 mL
1 cup	dry red wine	250 mL
	Finely grated zest of 1 lemon	
1/2 cup	pitted prunes, snipped into thirds	125 mL

Sponge cake

1/4 cup	dry bread crumbs	50 mL
4	eggs, separated, at room temperature	4
1 tsp	vanilla extract	5 mL
3/4 cup	granulated sugar	175 mL
Pinch	salt	Pinch
1/2 cup	all-purpose flour	125 mL
1/2 cup	potato flour *or* cornstarch	125 mL
	Icing sugar for dusting	

1. In a small saucepan over medium heat, dissolve sugar in red wine. Add lemon and snipped prunes; reduce heat to low and let simmer about 20 minutes or until all the liquid has been absorbed. Allow to cool.

2. Scatter bread crumbs over surface of prepared pan. Shake the pan to remove excess.

3. In a bowl using an electric mixer, beat egg yolks with the vanilla. Add half the sugar and whisk together until light and frothy, about 5 minutes. In another bowl, sift together the flour and potato flour.

4. In a large bowl, beat egg whites with the salt until soft peaks form. Gradually add remaining sugar, beating until firmer peaks are formed. Using a rubber spatula, fold the egg yolk mixture into the egg white mixture. Sift the dry ingredients over the egg mixture and fold in.

5. Pour cake batter into prepared cake pan and smooth the surface. Arrange the soaked prunes on top and bake in preheated oven for about 45 minutes or until the sponge cake is firm to the touch and pale golden. Turn sponge out onto a rack to cool. Dust with icing sugar before serving.

MAKES ABOUT
4 DOZEN

This name usually refers to the chewy, almond macaroon-type biscuits that are imported from Italy, individually wrapped in thin tissue paper and packed in those beautiful decorative tins. However, these amaretti (which translates as "little bitter things") are Sicilian in origin and resemble nutty little biscuits, perfect with a steaming latte or to accompany fresh peaches.

Egg whites will whip to stiff peaks faster when not ice cold.

Amaretti

Almond Biscuits

PREHEAT OVEN TO 325° F (160° C)

NONSTICK COOKIE SHEETS OR REGULAR COOKIE SHEETS LINED WITH PARCHMENT PAPER

2 cups	whole unblanched almonds, toasted	500 mL
1 1/4 cups	granulated sugar	300 mL
2 1/2 tbsp	all-purpose flour	33 mL
1/4 tsp	salt	1 mL
4	egg whites, at room temperature	4

1. In a food processor or blender, combine toasted almonds, sugar, flour and salt; process on and off until the mixture resembles very fine, powdery crumbs.

2. In a large dry bowl, beat the egg whites with a pinch of salt until stiff peaks form. Fold in ground-almond mixture until well blended.

3. Using a 1-tsp (5 mL) measure, mound batter onto the cookie sheets, 2 inches (5 cm) apart. Bake in preheated oven for about 20 minutes or until golden brown. Allow to cool, then transfer to a rack to cool completely. Store in an airtight container.

SERVES 6 TO 8

*Also called Siena cake, this
rich, dense confection must be
served in ultra thin slices. I like
to arrange overlapping slices of
it on a serving plate drizzled
with a little thinned custard or
cream. The addition of chocolate is not traditional but delicious nonetheless. Makes a
lovely gift at Christmas.*

Pan Forte di Siena

Fruit and Nut Cake

PREHEAT OVEN TO 400° F (200° C)

**9-INCH (23 CM) SPRINGFORM CAKE PAN, LINED WITH
PARCHMENT PAPER**

8 oz	hazelnuts, skins removed, roasted	250 g
8 oz	almonds, skins removed, roasted	250 g
1/2 cup	dried apricots, finely chopped	125 mL
1/3 cup	candied pineapple, finely chopped	75 mL
1/3 cup	mixed candied peel, finely chopped	75 mL
1/3 cup	candied citron, finely chopped	75 mL
1 1/2 cups	all-purpose flour	375 mL
1/4 cup	cocoa	50 mL
2 tsp	cinnamon	10 mL
4 oz	semi-sweet chocolate	125 g
1 cup	honey	250 mL
3/4 cup	sugar	175 mL

1. In a bowl stir together hazelnuts, almonds, apricots, pineapple, peel and citron.

2. In a bowl set over a saucepan of simmering water (or in a microwave), melt chocolate. In a heavy saucepan, combine honey and sugar; bring to a boil, then simmer for 5 minutes.

3. Add honey mixture and melted chocolate to the nut-fruit mixture; combine well with a wooden spoon. Transfer batter to prepared pan and smooth down with the back of a spoon.

4. Bake in preheated oven for 20 to 30 minutes, or until firm to the touch but still soft in the center. Cool completely before thinly slicing. (The cake firms up as it cools). Store in an airtight container.

Along with the more famous gelati, fruit granite are enjoyed all over Italy in little espresso bars and shops. They are very easy to make and don't require any special equipment. This lemon version is remarkably refreshing at the end of a meal or as a palate-cleaner between courses. I enjoyed this in the south of Italy where it is made using enormous, intensely flavored Meyer lemons.

Granita al Limone

Lemon Ice

1 cup	sugar	250 mL
2 cups	freshly squeezed lemon juice (about 8 lemons)	500 mL
	Fresh mint sprigs	

1. In a heavy saucepan over medium heat, combine sugar with 2 cups (500 mL) water. Bring to a boil, stirring, until sugar is dissolved. Remove from heat and allow to cool completely.

2. Using a fine sieve, strain lemon juice into cooled syrup and stir to blend well. Pour mixture into a shallow ceramic or glass dish and place in freezer. As it starts to freeze (about 20 minutes), use a spatula to scrape and stir ice crystals forming around the edges into the middle until a uniform grainy consistency is reached.

3. Scoop into tall glasses and serve garnished with fresh mint.

Index